CABIN CREEK CHRONICLE

The History of the Most

Remote Ranch in America

G. WAYNE MINSHALL

ISBN: 978-0-9849490-1-4
Library of Congress Control Number: 2014932363

1. Western US History. 2. Wilderness. 3. Homesteading. 4. Adventure.
5. Self-reliant Living (lifestyle). 6. Idaho. 7. Frank Church River of No
Return.

PRINTED IN THE UNITED STATES OF AMERICA

PREFACE

Even in the 1930s, Jean and Merl Wallace regarded their place on Cabin Creek, deep within Big Creek country in central Idaho, as the "most remote ranch in America." At the time, it was still almost 100 miles from the end of the nearest paved road and, even in the best of times, the final 30 miles were accessible only by horseback, dogsled, or on foot. Though they did not realize it, their ranch and the surrounding country was central to an important segment of Idaho history and was to become a key element in one of the nation's first designated primitive and wilderness areas. The story of how their "Flying W Ranch" came to be, their struggles to keep it going, and its unexpected end is an account of what it takes to eke out a living in a setting where nature holds the upper hand. The very remoteness that drew them to the area and tested them to the limits of their abilities and beyond, ultimately would protect it from roads and irreversible development and come to be regarded as a treasured national asset to be preserved for future generations. But before that the Flying W would undergo transformation and consolidation in an effort to lessen its isolation, mute its wildness, and make life there less rigorous and more financially viable.

Cabin Creek is a medium-sized stream that feeds into Big Creek in the heart of the Frank Church River-of-No-Return Wilderness (subsequently referred to simply as the Frank Church Wilderness). Beginning in 1988, and extending over the next quarter of a century, my colleagues, students, family members, and I studied the ecology of Big Creek and some of its tributaries. In the course of this endeavor, I came to know intimately Big Creek country and its past, particularly as concerns Cabin Creek, a location where the country and its history intersect most profoundly.

I first encountered Big Creek while on a raft trip down the Middle Fork of the Salmon River in the summer of 1978. Its crystalline waters held their own against the blue-green of the Middle Fork for about a half mile, before the two united and tumbled their way another 19 miles confined between the towering walls of "Impassable Canyon" before joining the main Salmon River. At the time, I was struck by Big Creek's relatively large size and the abundance of leaves, pine needles, and other coarse debris — features unexpected for a stream almost 50 miles from its source. I vowed to come back some day to explore the basin and try to unravel this enigma. However, it was another decade before I would return, this time on foot with a research team, loaded backpacks, and several pack horses to carry our research equipment and supplies. It was on that 15-day expedition that we first waded though the waist-high grass of Cabin Creek Flat and forded the knee-deep brook from which it derives its name. Although I did not anticipate it at the time, in the years following I would get to know the area well and gradually discern its intriguing history in terms of individual lives, shifts in land use, and role in the establishment of one of the first and (outside of Alaska) the largest designated montane wilderness area within the United States. In this respect, the tale goes full circle from true wilderness, through a sequence of occupancies by an assortment of residents including the Wallaces, and eventually back to "wilderness." Thus the story of Cabin Creek provides valuable insights as to how the area's return to wilderness came about and to some of the tribulations and machinations faced by the inhabitants and the land in the process.

In a sense, this book is a sequel to the history of the first known white settlers on Cabin Creek, the Caswell brothers, that I have written about earlier in detail in my book *Wilderness Brothers*. Although the Caswells are included here as an integral part of the history of the area, the emphasis of this book is on the legacy they imparted to the place, especially in terms of structures and land use. Otherwise, the present account fills in the conditions and events before the Caswells' arrival, when the area was occupied by the Sheepeater Indians, who fought two engagements with the US Army. It then traces the history of the people who resided at Cabin Creek after the Caswells moved on, the kinds of land uses it was subjected to, and the significant events that occurred in relation to the site, both directly and indirectly.

The reader will readily discern an inconsistency in the level of treatment of different parts of the account. This is largely the result of a desire to adhere closely to the documented facts and to the type and level of detail within available written and photographic records. Though supplemented by an array of material from memoirs, reports, genealogical records, news clippings, and the like, the bulk of the account rests on three primary sources: (1) the unpublished diaries and autobiography of Luman G. Caswell, (2) the original Cabin Creek homestead records, and (3) the correspondence and other relevant papers of the former Cabin Creek residents Jean and Merl Wallace. Note that the dates in the subtitles of the chapters refer to the period of occupancy of the individuals at Cabin Creek but that the actual period covered may exceed that for purposes of continuity.

ACKNOWLEDGMENTS

I am extremely grateful to the good fortune and people, especially David Burns and Jim Akenson, that led me to the sources noted above and to my wife Judy for her active participation in assembling the information. I thank Cathy (Lanham) Gillihan for providing information about her father Rex and activities at Cabin Creek during his time there. Kindra Serr, in the GIS Center of Idaho State University, made the maps. In addition, I acknowledge the help and dedication of: James Barnes, Richard H. Holm Jr., Gayle Dixon, Larry Kingsbury, Holly Akenson, Julie Miller, and Jim Morris in providing information and photographs. In particular, Richard and Gayle are responsible for calling my attention to and making available many of the photographs used in assembling this book. Many other historic photographs and supportive history relevant to the area may be found in Holm's "Bound for the Backcountry: a history of Idaho's remote airstrips." Charles R. Peterson enhanced most of those photographs I have included, with the use of Adobe Photoshop Lightroom photo-editing software. Judy Minshall reviewed several versions of the entire manuscript, Bert Cushing reviewed major portions of an early version, and Gayle Dixon reviewed the Pre-settlement Era Chapter. All provided valuable comments and identified a variety of errors, which were corrected. Barry Rower designed the cover and text and formatted it into print-ready form.

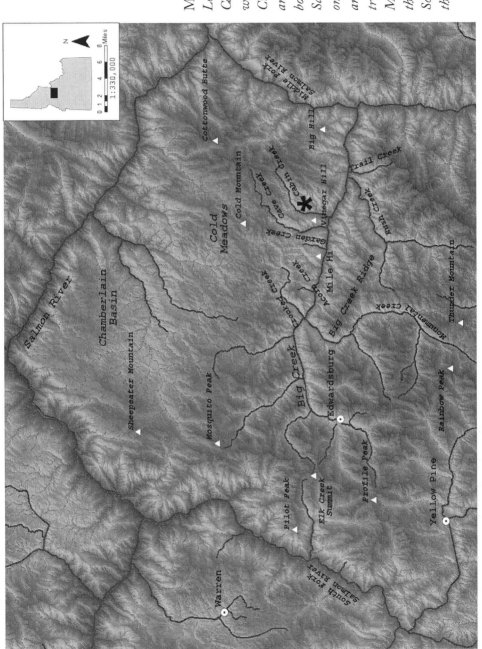

Map 1.
Location of Cabin Creek (*) within Big Creek country and vicinity, bounded by the Salmon River on the north and its principal tributaries, the Middle Fork on the east and the South Fork on the west.

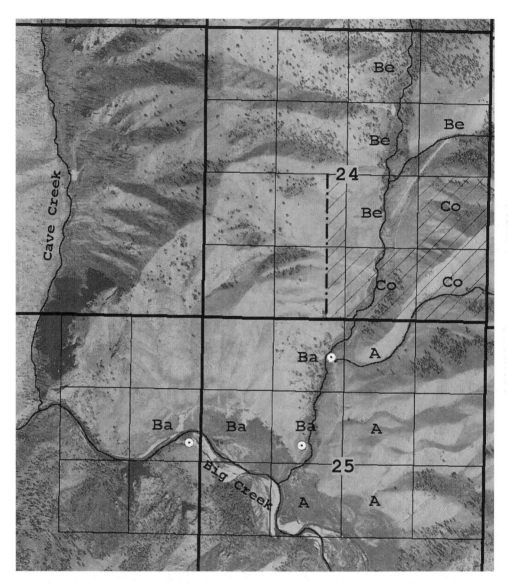

Maps 2a and 2b.
Aerial photograph of the main ranching area of Cabin Creek (a) with and (b)
without boundaries of the initial homestead patents. The core of the original
Caswell Ranch on Cabin Creek eventually was subdivided into four parcels
between 1910 and 1925, each within the 160-acre upper limit set by the federal
government for homesteads at that time. John Conyers was the last to own the

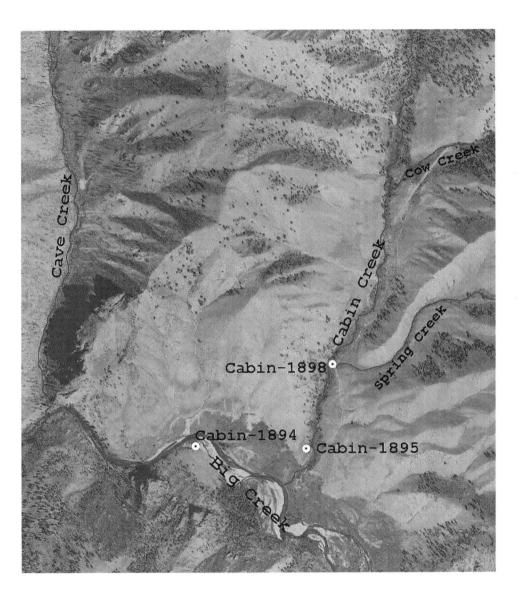

Caswell Ranch before it was subdivided into homesteads; later he filed on one of the subdivisions. As a result of the subdivision, three other names besides John Conyers' (Co) became prominent during this period: Orlando Mel Abel (A), his sister Sarah Elizabeth Bellingham (Be), and Archie C. Bacon (Ba). Later, Merl & Jean Wallace acquired the remaining 140-acre parcel (Co) situated between the Abel and Bellingham homesteads.

Contents

Frank Church River of No Return Wilderness viewed 7 June 2014 to the southwest in the vicinity of Camas Creek on a flight from Cabin Creek to Challis Idaho. Photograph by Charles R. Peterson.

⇜ The Setting ⇝

Through a combination of geography and chance, Cabin Creek has been at the center of several significant historical events in the development of Idaho Territory and, later, the State. In addition, its existence at the very fringe of inhabitancy highlights the challenges faced by pioneer prospectors and ranchers that continued midway into the 20th century, well past the time when most of the residents of the state and nation had become citified.

Cabin Creek first gained notice as the site of an embarrassing defeat of a detachment of the US Army by a small band of Native Americans. Many years later it became the base of operations for the Caswell brothers, who discovered a large deposit of gold two days travel away on the often snow-shrouded Thunder Mountain. Their discovery triggered the last major gold rush in Idaho and dramatically altered their lives, the lives of the "stampeders," and the ultimate fate of the central portion of the State. In succeeding eras of land ownership, Cabin Creek passed from unauthorized squatters to certified homesteaders and subsequent purchasers. In terms of land use, the inhabitants went from those who mainly lived off the land, in the sense of dependency on it and self-sufficiency from outside sources, to those who lived *off* the land in the context of living mostly somewhere else and deriving most of their subsistence from distant locations disconnected from the immediate landscape.

The Cabin Creek area lies astride what was long the main route between the gateway settlement of Warren, at the western fringe of Idaho's granitic core, and the bisecting incision and passageway made by the Middle Fork of the Salmon River. Thus it came to serve as a key node of communication and rare social interaction in this difficult terrain. Communication was first by word of mouth passed along by intermediaries at Cabin Creek; then by mail carrier traveling on foot, on horseback, or by dogsled to and from the site; later still by telephone and two-way radio; and finally occasionally even by airplane and satellite phone. It was a place to stop and visit, to receive and send mail and packages, and eventually to call from or to in time of need. It is not surprising then that many vignettes of backcountry life took place here from the mundane to the dramatic, through bone-wearying labor and discouragement to visible progress and hope, and from birth to violent death.

Initially the Cabin Creek "spread" was operated primarily as a livestock ranch and this mode of operation extended from the mid-1890s through the 1920s. However, from the outset and extending up to the early 1960s, life at Cabin Creek lacked most of the "creature comforts" taken for granted today. Even in the relative comfort of a snug double-roofed, well-chinked log cabin, residents at Cabin Creek had to endure a number of challenges to which people today are totally oblivious. These center around the absence of indoor plumbing, central heating, lighting at the flip of a switch (in multiple locations/rooms), and means of distant two-way communication. Most current residents of developed countries such as the United States, Canada, and the British Isles have not experienced and cannot imagine extended periods beyond a few hours without flush toilets, unlimited hot water on demand, thermostatically controlled heating and cooling constantly available in all or most rooms, and extended means of voice or text communication by means even as "primitive" as land-line telephone. The absence of these were everyday realities to most of the inhabitants of Cabin Creek.

Eventually, the site transitioned into two of the first dude ranches in Idaho, beginning about the time of the establishment of the Idaho Primitive Area in 1931 and continuing to develop until a few years before the area's incorporation into the Frank Church Wilderness in 1980. The site ultimately included hydroelectric power, indoor plumbing, airplane service, and motorized local transportation. Following designation of the wilderness by Congress, the Cabin Creek area was cleansed of most traces of human occupation and returned to a reasonable semblance of the way it was over a century before, when the lone structure that first provided the area its name was built.

EXCEPT FOR A single-lane dirt track extending along the Magruder Corridor between the Montana border and Elk City, no roads cross the central region of Idaho — as a result of masses of mountains in the way. Only a single loop of linked highways encircles this core like a loosely fitting beaded bracelet. Midway down, this pavement-bounded area is subdivided into roughly two halves by the east-to-west-flowing Salmon River. The northern half is drained mainly by the Lochsa and Clearwater Rivers and the southern section primarily by the Salmon. It is in this latter portion of topography that Cabin Creek is located.

The main Salmon River, from its headwaters near Galena Summit (8990') northwest of Sun Valley, flows northward for some 195 miles, or roughly half its total length, before veering sharply westward across the state at its juncture with the North Fork. On the west side of the Main Salmon during its south to north excursion are its chief tributaries, the Middle and South Forks, which join the Main about one-quarter and three-quarters of its distance across the state. The valley of the Salmon from Galena to North Fork is relatively wide, having been fashioned in part by ancient glacial action. But the valleys of the Middle and South Forks follow geologic fissures unworked by glacial activity and hence strongly confined by steep mountain and canyon walls. Within this vast expanse of deeply-dissected mountains and rapid, narrowly-confined rivers, lies Big Creek and its feeder stream Cabin Creek.

The valley of Cabin Creek is remote. Even today it is largely inaccessible to most people and its location in the middle of the largest montane wilderness in the contiguous United States emphasizes this fact. Historically it was even more isolated. In the 1860s when white settlers first entered what was then Idaho Territory, access to Cabin Creek was by trail 38 straight-line miles east of Warren. But because of the mountainous terrain, the tortuous route exceeded 70 miles and took several days of strenuous travel by horseback or on foot. It also entailed a nearly 4,000-foot drop in elevation from Warren Summit to the South Fork of the Salmon River and an arduous

Elk Creek basin and summit (top, left of center)viewed from the west rim of the South Fork of Salmon River. Photograph courtesy of the Payette National Forest.

5,690-foot climb in elevation up Elk Creek to its 8,670-foot pass before descending steeply again to intercept the turbulent waters of Big Creek. Of the entire journey, the 30-mile section encompassing the sharp descent to and ascent from the South Fork(whether coming or going) was the most arduous and required the most careful staging of overnight camp sites.

Upon crossing Elk Creek Summit, one enters the 595 square mile watershed of Big Creek. Though starting as a medium-sized "creek," the stream attains river status about where Monumental and Crooked Creeks join it from opposite banks 23 miles from Elk Summit. Both sides of the route down Big Creek are lined by precipitous mountains rising several thousand feet above the valley bottom. Some of the more notable ones on the north are Wolf Fang (9,007'), McFadden Point (8,551'), Ramey (8,383'), Cold Mountain (8,084'), and Black Butte 8,711').

Standout pinnacles to the south include Center Mountain (9,323'), Rainbow (9,325'), Lookout (8,680'), Mormon (9,545'), and Two Point (9,426'). Big Creek Ridge, which is made up of a number of lesser peaks, parallels Big Creek along its southern flank over much of the river route between Monumental and Rush Creeks. Bordering the route down Big Creek on the north and set back some distance from this mountainous fringe are high, rolling plateaus and low ridges in the Chamberlain Basin and Cold Meadows regions. These include expansive wet meadows such as Chamberlain, Cold, Crescent, Hand, Moose, and Meadow of Doubt. Apart from the meadows, bare rock on steep slopes, and sagebrush-grass vegetation on dry exposures, the area is forested. At higher elevations, dense stands of lodgepole pine and Douglas fir are common, together with some Engelmann spruce and limber pine. At

Upper Big Creek basin. Photographed facing south from McFadden Point, with Goat Mountain in the back on the left and Logan Mountain on the right. Big Creek flows toward the viewer on the left, separated from the elevated meadow of Big Creek Flat by a ridge or "Hogback." Logan Creek and Government Creek enter from the right at the upper end of the meadow and join Big Creek near the lower end of the Hogback. The former Edwardsburg and Big Creek Village and original Big Creek Ranger Station were located near the upper end of the meadow. Photograph by Bob Dustman.

(Above) William and Annie Edwards in front of their home in Edwards-burg [prior to 1927]. Photograph from Dave Lewis Special Collection (MS Accession #2011-03), University of Idaho Library. (Below) Remains of home and attached buildings which subsequently morphed into the main part of the burg (left to right: grocery store, post office, room & boarding house, unknown). Photograph July 2012 by author.

lower elevations, especially along Big Creek and the Middle Fork of the Salmon River, there are mature Ponderosa (western yellow) pine.

Big Creek Village seen in the early 1950s consisting of a residence, hotel, store, and auto-shop with gas pump (from left to right). Photograph by Bob Dustman. The hotel and store have since burned to the ground.

There was no settlement in the Big Creek basin until the early 1900's when a small cluster of buildings beside part of a large meadow known as Big Creek Flat gave rise to Edwardsburg (originally called Logan). In 1904, William A. Edwards brought his wife Annie (Napier) Edwards and 5 year old son from Spokane and built the first home there. Both William and his wife were in their mid-30s at the time. He had been an Assistant Attorney General in the Department of Interior in Washington, DC, specializing in mining law, until 1901 when his health failed and he headed west to seek an outdoor life. Annie also was well educated and graduated with honors from Wesleyan University.

Two decades after the Edwardses' arrival the Idaho National Forest established the Big Creek Ranger Station, known locally as "Headquarters," about a mile further north of Edwardsburg. Shortly after the founding of Edwarsburg, the residents gained access to the outside by way of a newly constructed wagon road, which went up Government Creek 11 miles to Elk Summit and then on to Warren. The road was made suitable for motorized traffic about the same time the ranger station was built. It wasn't until 1933 that an alternate route from Yellow Pine over Profile Summit was completed and by this time Edwardsburg was replaced by a small cluster of buildings located nearer the ranger station, eventually consisting of a general store, a small hotel, and an automotive repair shop and gas station. The new road to Big Creek Village, over Profile Summit to Yellow Pine and connecting to Cascade, was much closer to a reasonable-sized town and railhead (Cascade) than the route over Elk Summit to Warren and McCall and greatly simplified overland travel to the outside and purchases of supplies. Soon the mail also began arriving via this direction. Eventually, the road was extended from the Village, down Big Creek to the Snowshoe Mine on Crooked Creek. However, the segment to Yellow Pine was open to motorized vehicles only during the snow-free season. In 1936, when the hotel was built, a postoffice was established in the store, officially giving rise to the village of Big Creek until the postoffice was discontinued at the end of 1951. In autumn 2008, three of the buildings: a log residence and the hotel and general store, which had been merged in more recent times to become the "lodge," were destroyed by a fire presumed to have originated in the chimney of the lodge.

Although Yellow Pine is closer to "civilization" from Edwardsburg or Big Creek village than Warren, it still is 60 miles on what at that time was a rough winding road to the nearest railhead and to pavement at Cascade. Both routes are closed by deep snow in the winter and the Edwardsburg area still is effectively isolated from all travelers, except those arriving on foot, by snowmobile, or by bush plane, from about the end of October until Independence Day (though in the 1930s the road from Yellow Pine often opened a month or so earlier). Even after Edwardsburg was reachable by road, 30 miles of travel by trail to Cabin Creek remained.

The US Forest Service was established in 1905 and the Idaho Forest three years later, but Big Creek Country was not included in the national forest reserve system until 1919. However, the first ranger stations in the closely-allied districts of Chamberlain and Cold Meadows were built in 1906 and 1913, respectively. It was several years more before the US Forest Service entered the Big Creek backcountry in a substantial way. In 1923 a tent camp was erected at Big Creek Flat just north of Edwardsburg to accommodate the newly created ranger district. Permanent structures, consisting of a combination ranger's office and commissary and a dwelling, were erected in 1924-1925. In those days, it was common for a ranger to spend almost his entire career at a single assignment. This was the case for Dan LeVan, who was Big Creek District Ranger from 1925 to 1950.

In 1944, two-thirds of the way through his term, the Idaho Forest was incorporated into the Payette Forest. As part of the reorganization of the Forest Service following World War II, the duration of service for Big Creek rangers was shortened to a few years each. For example, Ted Koskella, LeVan's successor, served only five years and Koskella's replacement Bob Burkholder was Big Creek Ranger for only about two years. However, following that, Earl Dodds served as Big Creek District ranger for another atypically long term from 1958-1984, during a critical transition period for the district when continuity was especially important. In addition to the post-WW II shift to the generally shortened tenure of district rangers, starting sometime prior to the winter of 1940-1941, they no longer resided year 'round at Big Creek but occupied the station only during the snow-free period from about mid-May through October. These changes tended to result in reduced familiarity of the rangers with the forest resources and with the private residents. They also were accompanied by the imposition of further regulations on resident *permitees* dependent on using Forest Service land under special permit for grazing their stock. For example, beginning about 1950, the Forest Service began enforcing a policy of removing any unusable stock, doing away with horse breeding (i.e., removing or castrating all mature stallions), and requiring one ton of hay be available for each horse wintered on Big Creek. This policy was discussed with all of the residents and set up as a 3-year grace period to try to reduce any hardship on them but it still further constrained their operations and worked in favor of externally-funded owners.

Cabin Creek Flat, as viewed from the air in May 2009, facing southwest up Big Creek. Photograph by author.

Acorn Creek Ranch, as seen in 1972, was occupied at various times by George Yardley, the John Routson family, Walt Estep, Phil Beal, the Dewey Moore family, and others. Photograph courtesy of the Payette National Forest.

Trail (now Pioneer) Creek, occupied at various times by John Conyers, Dave Lewis, Jess Taylor, and the University of Idaho Wilderness Research Station. Photograph by Charles R. Peterson May 2007.

CABIN CREEK JOINS Big Creek two-thirds of the way along the latter's approximately 60-mile course, about 38 miles from Elk Summit. Cabin Creek is situated midway between two other important nodes of human interaction along Big Creek: Acorn Creek 8 miles upstream and Trail (now renamed Pioneer) Creek 6 miles downstream. Below Edwardsburg, Big Creek generally flows within narrow canyons or steeply inclined valley-walls but at these three locations its valley widens sufficiently to accommodate meadows suitable for hay production and with entering tributaries for watering them and irrigating adjacent fields. Thus the deltas formed by Acorn and Trail Creeks also are particularly attractive locations for settlement and social interchange. Of these three

Cabin Creek Flat in July 2009 facing easterly with Horse Mountain looming in the background. Photograph by author.

sites, the confinement of Big Creek is least pronounced at Cabin Creek Flat. The ensuing meadow, some 100 acres in extent, currently resembles an African savannah with a few cottonwoods and shrubs fringing the otherwise grass-covered plain. In August 1879, Private Hoffner observed a similar scene but with more tall willows and cottonwood along the creek. When the Caswells arrived in the area, conditions apparently were much the same as the soldiers had encountered, with abundant growths of tall willows and mature cottonwoods. Present-day conditions differ, harboring few shrubs and mainly grass, largely due to shifts in land use, brought about by non-Indian occupants over the succeeding 135 years.

Cabin Creek enters the Flat from the north after flowing several miles through a broad valley fringed by sagebrush-covered foothills that rise steeply and, on the east side of the creek, eventually meet the surrounding forested mountains. A smaller portion of meadow lies across Big Creek to the south, beyond which the foothills are dispensed with and the terrain rises sharply to the mountain ridgetops. These more-moist slopes were populated with a continuous, dense stand of conifers until they were killed by fire and drought around the year 2000. The full expanse of this forested mountainside provided the view from the front door of the Caswells' cabin during their first year of residence.

About a mile up Cabin Creek from its mouth, a narrow strip of foothill coming off Horse Mountain from the east pinches the stream against the foot of Vinegar Hill and obscures the view of the big meadow. A small, crystalline springbrook also runs along the base of the foothill on the north and enters Cabin Creek here.

Cabin Creek basin, as seen facing north from an approaching plane in 1966, starting with the northern edge of Cabin Creek Flat at the bottom. Photograph courtesy of the Payette National Forest.

Upstream of this constriction, with Cabin Creek still hanging against the base of Vinegar Hill, the valley broadens sufficiently to contain an irregular strip of land that, like the Flat, invites development for ranching or farming. This widened portion together with Cabin Creek Flat constitute the largest expanse of arable land along Big Creek. Also, because of its relatively low 4100-foot elevation and north-south orientation, it has a long snow-free period and the most favorable growing conditions of any place in the Big Creek basin.

Pre-Settlement Era

L ong before white men inhabited the land embraced by the Middle and South Forks of the Salmon River, a semi-no-madic band of Native Americans roamed the mountains and dwelled in the valleys. Archaeological evidence indicates that the area has been occupied for thousands of years. It is believed that the ancestors of these Shoshones, driven by a drying climate, migrated north from the central Great Basin into the region that now includes Idaho and Wyoming. The central Idaho band was a subgroup of Northern Shoshone Indians known as the Tukudika or Sheepeaters that eventually worked out a way of life that allowed them to remain year 'round in this rugged "Land of the Middle and South Forks" and subsist entirely on the resources it provided, perhaps to avoid conflict with more aggressive tribes found elsewhere.

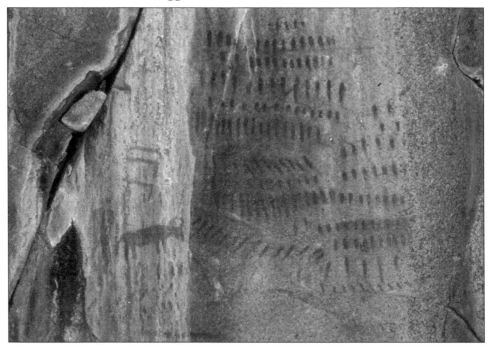

Pictograph from lower Big Creek. Presumably a tally of the number of Bighorn sheep harvested by Shoshone Indians. Photograph courtesy of the Payette National Forest.

15

For a long time dogs were an integral part of their lives, warning them of danger, carrying pack loads or hauling travois, and assisting in hunting. Even with the introduction of the horse in the 17th century, the life style of this resident group does not seem to have changed appreciably. They were hunter-gatherers and overall seem to have had little permanent impact on the land.

The Tukudika lived in temporary shelters called wickiups, conical-shaped dwellings, circular or oval at their base, and made of poles covered with branches, brush, and bark or later with canvas or blankets; sometimes wickiups were set over depressions or "house pits" up to 1 to 2 feet deep. The center of the floor was used for a fire. The wickiups were organized as small groups averaging four to six units, collectively housing 16 to 20 individuals, mainly family members. Winter was spent in the lower elevations for their more moderate weather conditions. Spring and summer were spent in meadows and along wide stream banks at the middle and then, as the snow left, upper elevations near small springs.

In the spring of the year, the people harvested bulbs, roots, grouse, small mammals such as rabbits and marmots, salmon, and

freshwater mussels. They especially prized Camas bulbs, biscuit root, and wild carrots (yampa), which they dug from the wet ground. Salmon were captured during their spawning runs by spearing and by the use of weirs or traps made from a combination of logs and willow shoots. During the cooler months of autumn

Remains of a wickiup. The original height has been reduced considerably by the rotting off of the poles at their bases. Photograph courtesy of Larry Kingsbury.

Shoshone hunting blind located on a talus slope where Bighorn were likely to be encountered. Photograph courtesy of the Payette National Forest.

and especially at the higher elevations, they hunted large herbivores including deer, elk, and moose but they were particularly adept at harvesting Bighorn sheep, which they shot from blinds with atlatls and darts and later with bows-and-arrows or captured in carefully engineered traps. Some of this meat may have been cut into thin strips and dried (as were fruits, berries, and fish) and stored for win-

A collection of projectile points from Big Creek basin used by the Sheepeater Indians to hunt game. Scale is 1 bar = 1 centimeter. Photograph by Frank Leonhardy courtesy of the Payette National Forest.

ter use. However, hunting probably persisted throughout the year and, during lean times, their bones were cracked to obtain the greasy marrow. Surprisingly there is very little evidence that they ate dogs or other canids. The Sheepeaters also tanned the hides of the animals they killed for food (as well as those from badger, coyote, fox, and wolf) to craft clothing and other useful articles.

The first known presence of white men at Cabin Creek was both contentious and short-lived and did not occur until the summer of 1879. It involved a brief encounter by a small contingent of the US Army with an even smaller band of Indians, who were camped at Cabin Creek Flat. From the opening of the area west of the Mississippi up until the mid-1870s, armed conflicts between whites and Native Americans in the northwestern interior of the United States were relatively rare. Then conflicts between the US Army and the Indians arose that were aimed at containment of the Indians and elimination of any further threat from them. The encounter at Cabin Creek was one of these.

The annexation of Texas in 1845, the successful outcome of the Mexican War of 1846-1848, and the resolution of the Oregon boundary dispute with Great Britain in 1846 generally are recognized as opening the lands west of the Mississippi to settlement by Americans of primarily Anglo- and other European origin. These events greatly facilitated the large-scale westward emigration of whites from the existing United States, that was fueled by the discovery of gold on the American River in northern California in January 1848. Although both the Oregon and California trails passed through what was to become Idaho, the influence of the emigrants and their limited settlement during the 1840s and 1850s was restricted to a narrow band mostly following the Snake River as it flowed on its way westward to join the Columbia.

Initially, prospectors and settlers traveling these trails or coming by sea concentrated along the Pacific Coast but after a dozen years they spread inland in sort of a reverse migration, as gold and other valued mineral deposits were discovered there. Some of these adventurers proceeded up the Columbia River. Among them were Elias Pierce and ten other men, who pushed past Walla Walla in Washington Territory, snuck past Nez Perce Indians on lands given them in 1855 under treaty with the United States, and discovered gold on Orofino Creek, a tributary of the Clearwater River. Soon several thousand prospectors, ignoring

Nez Perce treaty rights, occupied the area and established Pierce City in 1861. Lewiston, the entry port from the Columbia to the Clearwater, was established that same year. As the most promising ground was claimed and the claims ran out, the gold seekers pressed on south to other hot spots including Elk City, Florence, Dixie, and Warren. In addition, other gold seekers, having crossed Oregon by land or gone up the Snake River, pushed inland to the Boise (August 1862; Idaho City established October 1862) and Owyhee River Basins (spring 1863; Silver City established 1866). More-enduring settlement of the land was aided by enactment of the Homestead Act of 1862, which offered free land, and completion of the Transcontinental Railroad in May 1869.

Cessation of the Civil War in 1865 helped stoke this new surge of immigrants, drawn by the vast expanses and rich potential of the western frontier's resources. In 1866 only a handful of tribes still retained the ability and inclination to obstruct the westward movement. In the Rocky Mountains they were primarily the Bannock, Nez Perce, and Utes. These tribes, and others in the area, such as Sheepeaters and Paiutes, were nomadic or semi-nomadic and needed a great deal of country and its resources to sustain their way of life. As the white population became established and expanded, the open spaces essential to the Indians became more fragmented and shrunken in size. The availability of buffalo and other game and food supplies was drastically reduced, as were places for their horses to graze. As these pressures built, irritations and conflicts between the two factions increased and inevitably led to armed confrontations and to suppression by the US Army.

Brigadier General Oliver Otis Howard arrived at Fort Vancouver just across the Columbia River from Portland in September 1874 to take command of the area encompassed by the State of Oregon and the Territories of Washington and Idaho. Among the tribes Howard and his troops were responsible for overseeing, were the Bannock, Nez Perce, and Northern Shoshone all of which had a major presence in Idaho and immediately adjacent lands. Armed conflict erupted first with a portion of the Nez Perce tribe known as the "nontreaties." This group did not accept a new treaty in 1863 that rescinded and greatly reduced the size of the reservation set aside for them in 1855. The campaign against the Nez Perce was resolved in a series of running battles over a few tense months between summer and late fall in 1877. Next was the Bannock-Paiute War of 1878, which began May 30 on Camas Prairie 90 miles southeast of Boise and ended in July in western Oregon with the disbursement of Indian combatants.

Some of the Bannocks and Shoshones that eluded Howard's forces returned to Idaho and took refuge in the mountains of the Middle and South Forks of the Salmon River. The area already was occupied by bands of Sheepeaters who, although occasionally troublesome, usually did not bother the small number of whites in the area. The refugees spent the winter of 1878-1879 with the resident Sheepeaters. In February 1879, five Chinese prospectors were killed on Loon Creek, a tributary of the Middle Fork of the Salmon River. These killings were attributed to the Sheepeaters, although they denied this. Upon learning of the event in May, Howard dispatched Captain Reuben Bernard, 2nd Lt. Jno. Pitcher, and a troop of 56 men of the 1st Cavalry (Company G) from Fort Boise to travel northeast toward Loon Creek in search of the murderers. A slightly smaller force of 48 mounted 2nd Infantrymen and three officers (from Companies C & K) was sent southeast from Camp Howard, under command of Lieutenant Henry Catley. Supporting Catley was a 34-mule pack train with six civilian packers, including Dave Lewis, and two scouts Josh Faulkner and Dave Munroe.

Camp Howard was a temporary post near the adjacent villages of Mount Idaho and Grangeville. It was established in late July 1877 by Catley's unit, which had been sent out west from Atlanta, Georgia earlier in the month, at the end of the Reconstruction era. Included among the troops was a young private named Harry Eagan.

After Catley's forces set out from the camp, 2nd Lieutenants Edward S. Farrow and William C. Brown left Umatilla Agency July 7 with seven soldiers and 20 Indian Scouts. They crossed the Snake River at Brownlee's Ferry and eventually joined Bernard August 6 in Long Valley near the falls of the Payette River (present day Cascade); then both commands left for Johnson's Ranch located

*Cabin Creek Flat as viewed from the trail facing east down Big Creek,
with much the same perspective as the US Cavalrymen must have first seen
it in 1879. Photograph by Amanda Rugenski July 2004.*

between Warren and Elk Creek Summit at the mouth of Elk Creek
on the South Fork of the Salmon River. It was during these actions
against the Sheepeaters that the first recorded presence of white
men at Cabin Creek occurred.

A noted authority on the Indians and the army in the west,
Robert M. Utley (Utley 2003) generously characterized the
Sheepeater Campaign and challenges faced by the Army as ". . . a
war less against Indians — they probably mustered no more than
thirty fighting men — than against one of the most rugged wildernesses in North America." As Utley explained it "Towering mountains loom over canyons so deep and narrow that the sun lights
the bottom only at midday. Winter comes early and lingers late.
Although Bernard and Catley took the field in June, not until mid-
July did snowpacks melt enough to open a way to the heart of the
Sheepeater domain. Fallen timber obstructed the march through
the mountains, and cliffs and boulders made streams almost impos-
sible to follow. Stock gave out by the dozen [with many being carried downstream or rolling down mountainsides] causing the loss
of many rations and other supplies."

Bernard was unable to locate the Indians, but in late July Catley picked up an Indian trail leading east down Big Creek. On July 11 Catley's forces left Rains Ranch northeast of Warren, crossed the South Fork of the Salmon River and proceeded to Chamberlain Basin and then probably went down the future Garden Creek to Big Creek [Dave Lewis letter to W.C. Brown 1925, see below]. A few miles further down Big Creek on July 29, they reached the location of Cabin Creek Flat and found where a small group of Sheepeaters had recently been camped. In a February 1925 letter to William C. Brown [Archives of University of Colorado at Boulder Libraries: W. C. Brown 22-9], Dave Lewis wrote "I remember coming down Big Creek & camping about three miles above the mouth of Cave Creek. From there our scouts went down Big Creek to a point a mile below Cave Creek or near Cabin Creek & saw the Indians setting fish traps on the riffles. By the time our company moved that far down the creek the Indians had discovered our presence & moved down the creek. We came in contact with them about a mile or more

Vinegar Hill from across Cabin Creek Flat viewed facing northwest. In 1879, the soldiers retreated from the gorge to the rear of the photograph, across the Flat, and up the prominent steep slope on the left. Photograph by Amanda Rugenski July 2004.

(Above) Upstream view of Big Creek facing westerly from the cave at the mouth of Cave Creek. (Below) Cave at the mouth of Cave Creek with downstream view of Big Creek. Just beyond the bend, the river enters Cabin Creek Flat. Photographs by Amanda Rugenski.

Shoshone "sign post" on lower Big Creek. Inset shows close up of pictograph in the center of the main photograph. Photograph by Richard H. Holm Jr.

below the mouth of Cabin Creek. What is now called the First Ford." Although Dave Lewis mentioned Cabin Creek in his 1925 letter, the soldiers made no mention of its name in their diaries or of any structures, such as a cabin, being present at the time.

Catley and his troops pursued the Indians into the canyon beyond the meadow without posting an advance guard, while the pack train and rear guard remained behind. About two miles into the canyon, at a particularly constricted place along Big Creek the soldiers referred to as "the first crossing" and that now is known as "the gooseneck," the force was ambushed by about 5 Indians hidden in the rocky cliffs that pressed in on the river. Almost immediately, Private William A. R. Holm was wounded in his left foot and Private James Doyle was shot in his left forearm and thigh. Caught in the open by surprise and lacking decisive leadership, the troopers took cover behind willows and other shrubs as they continued to exchange fire with the Indians. Later, with the wounded on stretchers, they retreated to Cabin Creek where they met the pack train and spent an uneasy night.

The next morning it was decided that, to try to avoid any further encounter with the Sheepeaters, the troop would ascend a steeply sloping ridgeline running north along the west side of Cabin Creek, where they might escape to Cold Meadows and return to Camp Howard. However, as they moved up the ridge on what would come to be known as Vinegar Hill, one or more Indians got ahead of them by going up Cabin Creek and then up to a saddle where the soldiers were intercepted and fired upon. Thus intimidated, Catley ordered his men to fall back to the promontory they had just left and to take cover as best they could. Here, the soldiers exchanged a half dozen shots with the Sheepeaters, who then torched the surrounding sagebrush- and grass-covered hillsides to try to burn them out. Disaster was averted by building backfires and a change in the direction of the wind.

The soldiers spent the rest of the day on a hot hillside far from a source of water. Whether or not they were left with only vinegar to quell their thirst, as tradition holds, the unpleasant experience, which itself left a sour taste in their mouths, probably is what gave rise to the name Vinegar Hill. The men endured a long, sleepless night and around 2 a.m., after the moon set, they snuck down the steep backside of the ridge to Cave Creek, abandoning much equipment, supplies, and even clothing and losing a dozen fully-loaded mules in the confusion and panic. They made good their escape to Cold Meadows and headed for home. However, on their way back, Catley was stopped in the vicinity of Warren and redirected back toward Big Creek. Captain Albert G. Forse, who together with another officer and 23 of his own 1st Cavalrymen had been dispatched from Camp Howard after hearing of Catley's defeat, intercepted Catley and together they headed back to Big Creek to pursue the Indians. A court-martial later convicted Catley of misconduct, but President Hayes set aside the sentence of dismissal from the service.

Bernard, Farrow, Catley, and Forse's troops, now totaling about 160 men, linked up at Johnson's Ranch on August 10-12 and, with Farrow's scouts as advance guard, headed up Elk Creek on the 13th for where Catley had found the Indians. As they made their way down Big Creek, they noted numerous wickiups scattered along its banks and an occasional fish trap, indicating regular use of the area by Indians. Six days later, about 10 miles downstream from Cabin Creek, the Umatilla scouts made a surprise attack on a Sheepeater camp of 10 wickiups and captured its contents, including much of Catley's lost baggage, but the inhabitants escaped. The camp was located on an elevated bench above Big Creek and the troopers elected to stay there that night. The next morning the main force left to pursue the Indians but the Indians retaliated by attacking the supply train that was still forming and only lightly guarded.

During this skirmish Private Harry Eagan was severely wounded by a shot from a Spencer carbine. Apparently one or both of his femoral arteries were severed by the shot and, in a futile attempt to save him, one of his legs was amputated. Eagan

Soldier Bar, location of the second encounter of the US Army and their Umatilla Indian scouts with the Sheepeater Indians on August 19, 1879, viewed facing west along Big Creek. The "bar" is a terrace about 590 feet above Big Creek, that drops off steeply to the right (stream side) of the photograph. The burial site of Private Harry Eagan, who was mortally wounded during the encounter, is located in the clump of conifers lining the edge of the drop off near the narrow east (left) end of the bar, Photograph by Charles R. Peterson June 2013.

was buried in a shallow grave on the bench, which later was named Soldier Bar in his memory. His 39 year-old widow Kate and 7 year- old daughter were left in Mount Idaho to mourn his death without the benefit of a body to provide closure. After his death, Kate worked as a laundress to help cover her living expenses. Dave Lewis also was present that day. Dave would return to the area three decades later to reside and hunt mountain lion, bear, and big game. In the 1920s he would still remember the location of Harry's grave and help erect a monument over it.

The attack on the pack train was repulsed and the Indians scattered through the mountains. Lacking a trail to follow, short on rations, and about worn out, the troops were allowed by General Howard to call off the campaign. Bernard returned to Boise by way of the Middle Fork and Loon Creek. Catley and Forse returned to Camp Howard via Big Creek and Warren. However, Farrow secured Howard's permission for one last try at rounding up the enemy. On September 16, after obtaining fresh supplies in Warren, Farrow and Brown and their Umatilla Scouts proceeded via Rains Ranch and Chamberlain Basin in a southeasterly direction toward the Middle Fork. The scouts picked up a trail five days later and captured two Indian women, a boy, and an infant that then were used as bait to capture the rest of the band. Finally, on October 1 and 2, a total of 51 Sheepeater men, women, and children [of which only about 15 were warriors] and their chief Tamanmo (Warjack) drifted into Farrow's camp and surrendered. They were taken to Fort Vancouver and waited there the next summer while Farrow and five of their members returned to the Middle Fork region to search for any remaining holdouts. Then, in the summer of 1881, the Sheepeater prisoners traveled by boat and train to the Fort Hall Reservation in southeastern Idaho Territory, near present day Blackfoot.

When Farrow and his men left the area with the Sheepeaters, Native American occupation of the Middle and South Fork country effectively ended. Although a few trappers and prospectors probably ventured in occasionally and lived there temporarily on a seasonal basis, the region remained devoid of year 'round residents for about another decade. The first known record of white occupants on Cabin Creek did not occur until the autumn of 1894. Earlier that summer, Ben and Lu Caswell discovered gold in a tributary of Monumental Creek. In order to protect their find and be able to take advantage of the snow-melt runoff in the spring for sluicing, they decided to overwinter nearby. To do so, they needed to find a place at a lower elevation with milder conditions and abundant grass to keep their string of horses. In their search they stumbled onto the unoccupied flat at the mouth of Cabin Creek.

Although no longer a threat to white settlers, a remnant group of Sheepeaters apparently utilized the general area for at least another 35 years or so. In the mid-1920s, Francis Woods worked as a surveyor for the Forest Service and kept a series of work diaries. He wrote "The Salmon River Country is a vast and beautiful land and when I was mapping not many settlers were living there. Sometimes our survey party would encounter small bands of Indians still trying to live the old life of hunting and gathering. They didn't bother us and we didn't bother them. In a small way I could feel how much they loved the land and the free life because I too had come to love this land."

Lower Cabin Creek as it enters Cabin Creek Flat on Big Creek, less than ten years after it first was occupied by European settlers. Already evident is a network of irrigation ditches but the shrubby riparian vegetation (probably mainly willow) along the creek and the Flat is still relatively intact. Photograph by Luman G. Caswell courtesy of the Idaho State Historical Society (ISHS No. MS2/437.10).

The Squatters

In 1862, the Homestead Act made available surveyed, undeveloped federal land west of the Mississippi free to claimants willing to reside on the land and develop it. Even after the establishment of the Homestead Act, there was a considerable amount of government land in the western United States that could not be claimed for occupation because it had not been officially surveyed. The absence of official surveys usually stemmed from problems of accessibility and lack of public demand, associated with difficult terrain. Big Creek Country and much of the surrounding area in central Idaho fell into this category. For those who could find inhabitable locations suitable for farming or ranching within these areas, a common practice was to occupy the land and hold it by sheer presence and, if necessary, active defense. Often this was done in the spirit of homesteading and the belief that the occupier eventually would come to be recognized as the legal owner. In the mean time, transfers of such land from one party to another took place informally, often as a handwritten note signed by both parties and bearing the date of the transaction. These people came to be known as "squatters" and their claims to ownership were termed "squatters rights." In the late 19th century, in the country east of Warren, along the South Fork Salmon River and in the mountains beyond, this still was the principal or only means of ownership. Even before the Caswells arrived at Cabin Creek, some previous squatter had been there, built a cabin and left other evidence of extended occupation but nothing is known about who this was or exactly when it occurred. Therefore, the only recourse open to folks such as the Caswells was to occupy the land in good faith that the surveyor eventually would come and their presence would establish their right to own the land.

CASWELL BROTHERS 1894–1906

LUMAN CASWELL and his older brother Ben came to Idaho Territory in 1888, by buckboard and horseback from Colorado, in search of

Luman, Benjamin, and Daniel Caswell (left to right). Photograph taken by Myers Studio, Boise, ID and provided courtesy of the Idaho State Historical Society (ISHS #P1987.26.8).

their fortunes as prospectors. They spent several years in the vicinity of Big Bar and the Seven Devils Mountains along the western edge of the emerging state, with little to show for it. However, in the summer of 1894 they ventured east through the small town of Warren, crossed the steep-sided canyon of the South Fork of the Salmon River, and passed into the virtually unoccupied region of tall mountains and narrow valleys drained by Big Creek. This sharply fragmented, imposing country had long impeded travel and extended-habitation by early pioneers. A relatively short time later, as they made their way up Monumental Creek, a tributary to Big Creek, they discovered the first signs of the gold they were hunting. Incredibly, their search soon led them to the "mother lode" or, as they termed it, Golden Reef, that most prospectors dream of but never find. Because of the abundance of thunderstorms on the mountain where the Golden Reef lay, they came to call it "Thunder Mountain."

Lu and Ben returned to Warren and on August 22nd filed their first claims. They had not counted on such fantastic good fortune and were not prepared for an extended stay in the wilderness. Ben wanted to go back to their homestead on Big Bar and return the next summer, after the mountain passes reopened to horse travel. But Lu was worried about claim jumpers and wanted to stay closer to their find. They finally agreed to overwinter in the vicinity but first returned to Big Bar for supplies and to better equip themselves. Because of the high elevation and dense forest at Golden Reef, they needed to find a more hospitable location to keep their saddle horses and pack stock, with abundant grass and less snow and cold. By an added stroke of luck they stumbled onto Cabin Creek Flat and in December 1894 hastily erected a cabin on the south side of Big Creek, across from the main flat and facing Vinegar Hill. The cabin was about 26 feet long from north to south and 15 feet wide, with a sod roof and a stone fireplace. They may have chosen the location because it was on the same side of Big Creek as the trail to their claims or because of the presence of an existing cabin on the north side and a concern that the land surrounding it had already been claimed. Whatever the reason for the location of the first cabin, by the end of the following September of 1895, they had crossed the river and moved into the unoccupied cabin. That fall they fixed up the house, repaired the chimney, and dug a root cellar.

Ben and Lu Caswell's first cabin at Cabin Creek with a portion of the base of Vinegar Hill bordering Cabin Creek Flat in the background. Built in 1894; occupied over winter. Photographed circa 1901 by Luman Caswell, from an album owned by his grandson Stewart Taylor.

Subsequent investigation of their gold discovery by the brothers revealed that most of it, while "free milling" and thus not requiring difficult subsurface mining techniques, was in a very fine state. This required the development of a complex water-delivery system of reservoirs, ditches, and flumes; acquisition of hydraulic mining capabilities using hoses and a large nozzle or "giant;" and construction of an extensive set of sluice boxes, in order to capture and harvest most of the gold. All of this required time, extending over several years. After they harvested much of the more-easily available gold, they needed additional time to "shop around" their claims and entice a buyer with deep pockets to purchase them on the speculation that coarser, more plentiful "lode" gold lay buried below. As a result,

Site of Caswell 1895 cabin site and later of the Bacon family home. The cabin was located on the small flat in center of photograph just to the right of the shadow cast by the two fir trees. Outlines of the depressions of two root cellars are evident on the slope immediately behind the cabin site. The larger flat directly above the root cellars was the site of the Caswells' "upper garden." The trail crossing of Cabin Creek is between the two large clumps of willows on the lower right. Photograph by author.

The old Caswell blacksmith shop across Cabin Creek from their 1895 cabin and near the trail crossing, as it appeared shortly before it was destroyed by fire in 2000. Photograph by author.

the Caswells' main mining activities and occupation of Cabin Creek extended from 1894 to 1903.

By nature and necessity the Caswells were always "on the hunt" for game and fur bearers for both food and income. They shot large numbers of deer and Bighorn sheep for hides and food and trapped and poisoned mostly cougars and bears for furs. Initially the Caswells depended on the sale of large amounts of furs and hides and a small amount of gold to supply the cash needed for store-bought supplies and materials. This gradually reversed over the years and garden produce came to provide an added cash supplement. Also, it didn't take long after the brothers began to live in the wilderness year 'round, for them to realize that Ben was better suited for overseeing the mining operations and Lu better adapted for their ranching and farming needs. As a consequence, beginning in 1898, Ben spent most of his time (including winters) on Thunder Mountain and Lu spent most of his time at Cabin Creek, but with substantial amounts devoted to helping Ben during the late spring-early summer runoff period or transporting equipment and supplies from Warren and as far away as Boise.

The pre-existing cabin resided in by Ben and Lu Caswell starting the autumn of 1895 continued to be occupied until the autumn of 1898. It was located on a small bench along the west side of Cabin Creek that abuts Cabin Creek Flat and lies at the base of the main ridge coming down from Vinegar Hill. Both this bench and a slightly larger one a short distance uphill from it were served by an irrigation ditch. Lu's diary entries also suggest an existing road and means of conveyance prior to their arrival. In addition, there apparently was an existing blacksmith "shop" in a log building located on the bank just across the creek from the cabin. In late August 1897, their brother Dan arrived from Gardiner, Montana along with his good friend Wes Ritchey. All four men spent the winter of 1897-98 in the little cabin and it must have been almost more than they could bear. By the end, they were showing serious symptoms of boredom and stress and never tried it again. The experience also seems to have induced them to build another cabin.

The fully developed Caswell "Elkhorn Ranch" home place as it looked after it was sold to John Conyers. Photograph from Dave Lewis Special Collection (MS Accession #2011-03), University of Idaho Library. MG 190-6-50

In February 1898, Lu and Dan began building the new, larger cabin about 1/3 mile upstream and on the opposite side of Cabin Creek just above the valley constriction where it is joined by Spring Creek. It was finished and occupied by them that autumn and eventually became primarily Lu's place. Henceforth, Ben apparently overwintered on Thunder Mountain and Wes built a place a few miles further upstream on Buck Creek and across from an even smaller stream that later would be named Garden Creek, and joined up with a different group of prospectors. This left the new cabin for Lu and Dan. But in the winter of 1900-1901 Dan was on Thunder Mountain with Ben. Dan did not spend extended periods at Cabin Creek after that because he initially was needed for the accelerated mining activity on Thunder Mountain and later because the claims were sold. After the sale of their first set of claims (late 1901) Dan, Ben, and Wes left Big Creek Country but Lu stayed another two years. Dan and Wes both married in the spring of 1902 and Lu in September. Lu's new wife remained in Boise and he returned to the ranch at the end of January 1903. Soon after he got back, Lu began building a log addition to the 1898 cabin. It originally was planned as a bedroom for him and his wife. However, when he learned of her successful operation and that she would be able to have children, he modified the plans to include a second room to serve as a nursery. Lu left again in the autumn to be with his wife for the winter but his plans for them to live together at Cabin Creek never materialized.

Beginning around 1900, farm and ranch operations had expanded to the point that extra help was needed and "farm sitters" were hired to look after things while Lu was away. In Dan's place during the winter of 1900-1901, the Caswells' younger half-brother Cort and an old-timer Jonas Fuller stayed with Lu and helped him. Cort arrived in August 1900 and lived with Lu until May 1901. In mid April 1901, an old friend, John "Bull" Keffer, came over from his place on China Creek on the South Fork to help Lu, in exchange for room and board and pasture for his cattle, and stayed for the next 13 months. Jonas was a frequent visitor and helped out for extended intervals until he left the area around March 1903.

(Above) Sunken depression (mid right) marking the location of the Caswell root cellar beside Spring Creek as seen in June 2013 and (below) hand-

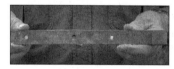

wrought strap-hinge found at the edge of the depression, that probably was made by Lu Caswell. Photographs by Charles R. Peterson.

US Mail delivery along Big Creek started in 1902 with the establishment of a post office in the new mining town of Roosevelt on Monumental Creek adjacent to Thunder Mountain. Previously the distribution point was Warren and the mail was carried by whomever happened to be going the right direction. Initially delivery from Roosevelt stopped at Cabin Creek but in February 1903, the mail route was extended another 6 miles to Trail Creek, where Bull Keffer and his two associates had a winter camp. At the time of the 1910 census, the mouth of Trail Creek apparently was being farmed by Francisco Stump (age 63) and his 36-year old son Francis. Shortly after, it became the home of Dave Lewis, Lu and Ben Caswell's former neighbor on Big Bar on the Snake River, and of John Conyers and his wife May.

Starting in 1898, all additional new structures built by the Caswells were in the vicinity of the 1898 Cabin, though the blacksmith shop, root cellar, and garden plot at the 1895 cabin site continued to be used. The old cabin was used for storage and also may have been occupied by Ben when he was around. In January-February 1900, they built a food storehouse (referred to as a "commissary" by later occupants). Initially it had a distinctive glass window in the door. By the time Lu left Cabin Creek and the ranch was sold, in addition to the 3-room ranch house and storehouse, there were a hillside root cellar to keep vegetables from freezing, a small log house over Spring Creek to keep milk and other foods cool in summer [though this may have been replaced with a larger structure by the next resident], a little shed with a sliding door next to the storehouse, a shop, a barn or stable for four horses, a hay shed, a calf shed, a chicken coop, and a powder house.

Scene along Cave Creek facing northeast at the site of a cabin occupied at various times by Charlie Meyers, Ed James, Gabe Homesly, and Wilbur Wiles. Photograph by author July 2004.

Over time, the area utilized by the Caswells expanded until the ranch operationally was over 1000 acres in size. The principal piece, extending along Cabin Creek and onto the Flat, accounted for about

600 acres. In addition there were Horse Mountain and the upper part of Spring Creek, an unclaimed part of the Flat on the opposite side of Big Creek, portions of Vinegar Hill, and a substantial expanse along Cave Creek. Cave Creek was named for a cave at its mouth, whose large, oval-shaped opening faced up Big Creek and was easily seen when coming down the river trail. The mouth of the creek was constricted and easily blocked off to prevent cattle from leaving but the valley then opened up to reveal a substantial amount of country suitable for grazing. Cave Creek and Horse Mountain were especially important for winter forage. The most productive area for hay and grazing was the Flat. The apparently pre-existing irrigation ditch that fed the garden plots associated with the 1895 cabin, originated from Cabin Creek and extended from above the entrance of Cow Creek, along the west side of the valley, to the 1895 cabin. Additional irrigation water came from Spring Creek and supplied the large field east of the 1898 cabin used for vegetables, an orchard, and berry bushes; the low bench above the cabin used for grain; the house garden; and the alfalfa field. In 1902 flow from Spring Creek was augmented by a "high ditch" originating from Cow Creek. This ditch was situated a good distance upslope of the valley bottom and passed along the east side for a mile or more before encountering Spring Creek. Though much smaller in size, the irrigated fields and patches used to grow grain, vegetables, and alfalfa were as important for the success of the ranch as the areas for grass hay and dryland grazing.

The Caswells' mounts, pack stock, and draft horses and skill in their use were essential to their independence and success

"High Ditch" built by Luman Caswell in 1902 originating from Cow Creek and augmenting water from Spring Creek for irrigating the east bench (grain) and lower (alfalfa) field. Composite from a series of photographs by Lynn Dixon in August 2005 also shows present-day landing field.

in the backcountry. For the first few years, the riding and pack stock were all the livestock raised at Cabin Creek and they pretty much had to fend for themselves for food and shelter. Lu and Ben cut their first hay using scythes and dug brush in the autumn of 1895 soon after getting established in the second cabin. Small amounts of hay also were harvested by scythe from the meadow in 1896 (probably) and 1897. There appears to have been a small increase in the amount harvested in 1898 but for the most part the livestock were simply allowed to forage at will, probably due in part to the lack of adequate fencing.

Another important and often overlooked component to the Caswells' survival and success at Cabin Creek was the availability of trees of assorted sizes and types in the adjacent forest. The most abundant and accessible source of this essential element was in the narrow canyon upstream of the entrance of Cow Creek about 3 miles north of the ranch house. Lesser forest stands, though less accessible, were present near the head of Spring Creek, along the west side of Cabin Creek below Cow Creek, and up Cow Creek. The trees, mostly conifers, provided logs, lumber, and shakes for buildings, poles for fences, and firewood for cooking and heating.

1899 marked the start of a major fencing effort and construction of a ditch off Spring Creek, east of Cabin Creek and the house, for irrigating the elevated flat near the new cabin. That year, a small amount (about 1½ acres) of supplemental feed, mainly oats, was grown on the elevated flat and this was expanded in subsequent years, as additional water became available from the high ditch, to 30 hundred weight in 1903. They also shocked up the straw to use for bedding and possibly for extra feed. Around the spring of 1900, they began to burn the meadow to remove the thatch, stimulate new growth of the grass, and eliminate some of the willow and other riparian shrubs. They also sowed some timothy hay that year. In 1902, they began to drain parts of the meadow and in 1903 undertook a major renovation of the Flat. In mid-1901, major improvements in their ability to process the grain and harvest the hay were made through purchase of a fanning mill for separating grain from chaff, a hay rake, and two mowers. The mowers apparently were unsatisfactory and in 1902 another was purchased and packed in, greatly increasing the quantity of hay harvested and requiring several men working for over two weeks to gather more than 10 wagon loads. In spring 1902, with the irrigation system for the field south of the ranch house along Cabin Creek in place and hay harvesting equipment available, Lu put in the first planting of alfalfa and harvested the first cutting (3 loads) the next summer. The construction of fences and development of the irrigation system were labor intensive and time consuming and once in place continued to extract a high tax in time and effort to maintain. The tradeoff may not have been worth it. After their own needs were met, whatever else was gained in production of crops and animal products for barter and sale may have been largely nullified by the added labor required and in enslavement to maintenance.

Throughout their time in the backcountry the Caswells relied heavily on wild game for meat, particularly deer and, like the Tukudika before them, Bighorn sheep. This was supplemented occasionally with grouse, salmon, and trout. Because of the availability of wild sheep, there never was a need to raise domestic ones and they also never raised pigs. Besides providing a source of income and serving as food, the large number of animals shot and trapped by the Caswells were used to bait their traps, make leather for clothing and lariats, craft stirrups and objects from horn, and for a myriad of other purposes. The first cows, chickens, and turkeys were acquired in the autumn of 1899. The following January, the old Dominique variety (dual purpose, medium size, black & white barred) hen laid what Lu claimed to be the first domestic egg produced on Big Creek. The first calves were born and butter churned in the spring of 1901. There were 22 head of cattle on the range by the fall of 1901. In addition, Lu began pasturing horses for friends and acquaintances from Thunder Mountain during the winter of 1901-1902. Lu and Ben probably arrived in 1894 with about a dozen head of horses. By 1902, Lu alone had about 10 packhorses, a couple of saddle horses, and two draft horses and, in addition, Ben and Dan had strings of their own. In 1902, besides the Caswell horses, there were 20 head of Caswell cattle, Bull's cattle (approximately 13 head) and horses, 13 horses of a man named Wood, and an unspecified number of horses belonging to Fuller & Roberts, Holcomb, and Nickelson.

The Caswells must have loved to grow vegetables and devoted a substantial amount of time to them. But it also was important for their subsistence and supplemental income. During their first spring in the 1895 cabin, Lu and Ben plowed the upper terrace, the "lower ground across the creek," and a garden patch next to the cabin. Although they fenced and planted the garden, it largely was neglected in 1896 because they were away most of the time prospecting or going out for supplies. However, they still harvested some vegetables that fall, including potatoes. In 1897, Lu and Ben plowed and planted the garden in late April-May and, in subsequent years, early to mid April generally marked the time of first planting. Lu specifically mentioned planting potatoes, carrots, and "vegetable oysters" (salsify) and irrigating in 1897. They probably also planted beets, radishes, onions, and turnips because they took seeds up to Thunder Mountain that year and planted some at their Burnt Flat cabin near the juncture of Mule and Monumental Creeks. In 1898, the area used for gardening was expanded by developing ground around the new cabin site. They also dug a new cellar there, southeast of the ranchhouse, to augment the one at the 1895 cabin. A relatively small garden patch on the east side of the new cabin was designated the "door yard" or house garden and soon was enclosed by a picket fence. Further east, there eventually was an orchard and probably additional garden space. Reference also was made to a "garden below house". That year Lu recorded the planting of cabbage, carrots, corn, lettuce, onions, potatoes, radishes, and turnips. There is no record of the contents of the 1899 garden other than potatoes but it probably was similar to the previous year.

In 1900, in anticipation of their own needs and those of other miners on Thunder Mountain, they expanded the garden tremendously in size and variety. Several kinds of plants, including cauliflower, peppers, and tomatoes, were started in cans in a newly constructed hotbed on the south end of the house, before being set out in the open. Over the course of three months, they planted beans, beets, cabbage (including over 100 Mammoth variety), carrots, cauliflower, corn, cucumbers, endive, kale, lettuce, onions, parsnips, peas (both coffee and vine), large amounts of potatoes, several varieties of radishes, rutabagas, salsify, summer squash, sunflowers, tomatoes, turnips, and watermelon. In several cases, such as with potatoes and onions, whole patches or fields were planted. In addition to vegetables, they set out plum trees and gooseberry, currant, and raspberry starts and tended an existing bed of strawberries. They also built a picket fence near the house that probably encompassed the house garden. 1901 was another big year for garden produce. In addition to the vegetables grown the previous year, cantaloupe, citron, collards, egg plant, two more kinds of squash (Hubbard & yellow), and both "yankee" and pop corn were raised. Only endive, lettuce, and parsnips were not mentioned but lettuce appeared again in 1903 and large amounts (2 acres) of parsnips were planted in 1902, so they may actually have been included.

The garden was expanded further in 1902 and acres of produce were grown. However, the variety decreased. Only celery was added and all of the new crops experimented with the previous year were discontinued in addition to cauliflower, kale, and watermelon. This list remained relatively constant the next (and final?) year except celery was dropped and cauliflower, cucumbers, lettuce and melons were reinstated. Separate patches/fields of carrots, beets, onions, and rutabagas were grown in addition to those in the house garden and on the bench above the 1895 cabin. Contrary to the growing of vegetables and berries, the first serious plantings of fruit trees did not occur until late in the Caswells' occupation of Cabin Creek. In 1902, two dozen each of plum and apple trees were started along with a peach and two pear trees. The next year, an additional 13 plum trees were put in.

The first exchange of garden produce was recorded in 1901 when Lu traded vegetables for flour with Elsie Taylor from Monumental Creek. But the market, both through barter and actual sale of vegetables, soon exploded. For example, in 1902 four pack-string loads totaling 2500 pounds of produce and several other loads of unspecified amounts were sold to buyers on Thunder Mountain alone. In May 1903, 13 packhorses and 1 mule laden with stored potatoes, parsnips, and onions from the previous year and several steers were taken to the new Dewey Mine and town of Roosevelt and sold. And in late September-early October, another 4425 pounds of produce was sent there.

The work of Lu Caswell and his helpers in the latter years of his residence at Cabin Creek, demonstrated the remarkable potential of the place to produce a great abundance and variety of garden crops. But never again in the history of the ranch would that potential even be approached.

Soon after the last load of vegetables departed in 1903, Lu left for Boise to be with his wife. He apparently never returned to Cabin Creek to stay. Lu hung onto the ranch for a couple more years as an itinerant owner and overseer but, when it became clear that his wife would not join him because of health and family reasons, he eventually sold out to John Conyers. In his unpublished autobiography written near the end of his life, Lu lamented that he never had it so good as when he was at Cabin Creek.

CONYERS 1906-1910

WHEN JOHN CONYERS acquired the Caswell ranch in 1906, he reportedly agreed to pay $3,000 for the land, buildings, and implements. He apparently made a $1,000 down payment but did not pay the remainder until he went to sell it in 1910. John originally came into Big Creek Country in the summer of 1902, at the start of the Thunder Mountain gold boom. He settled in what initially was the "tent city" of Roosevelt, which had sprung up along Monumental Creek, and set up a lavish saloon there at the north end of Main Street. He had divorced his first wife earlier and in May 1903 at age 44 married May Birdwell, a divorcee 10 years younger. May's 16-year old daughter Gussie was one of the witnesses at their Boise wedding. John and May rode the crest of the gold boom but in 1906, well ahead of the final demise of Roosevelt in May 1909, moved on down Big Creek to take up cattle raising on the former Caswell Ranch on Cabin Creek. They operated the ranch for four years, then paid off the remaining debt, and sold their "squatters rights" for the entire ranch to Orlando M. (Mel) Abel and John Routson. Nothing is known of activities at Cabin Creek during this time. The Conyers

The Trail Creek homestead about the time it was occupied by John & May Conyers and Dave Lewis. Photograph from Dave Lewis Special Collection (MS Accession #2011-03), University of Idaho Library.

seem to have maintained what the Caswells had put in place, though almost certainly at a reduced scale. Fortunately for the Conyers, they sold shortly before the area was opened for homesteading and the core of the original Caswell Ranch was divided into parcels with a maximum size of 160 acres each.

John Conyers, influential early resident of Big Creek country. Photograph courtesy of the Idaho State Historical Society (ISHS #72-120-42).

In the summer of 1910, the Conyers moved with some of their cattle six miles further down Big Creek to the mouth of Trail (Pioneer) Creek, where they remained until early-to-mid 1920. In doing so, they presumably took over the land and existing cabin formerly occupied by the Stumps. In 1911, they apparently were joined there by Dave Lewis, though they claimed separate residences at the time of the January 1920 Federal Census. However, a 1918 inventory of livestock and agricultural lands conducted by the Idaho National Forest listed only Lewis and not Conyers.

The Conyers probably knew Dave Lewis from the time they lived at Roosevelt during the Thunder Mountain Boom. Later, Dave visited them at Cabin Creek and helped with various chores, including gardening, along with another Roosevelt acquaintance Charlie Meyers. "Cougar Dave" Lewis had been through the area with the army in 1879 as a packer. Now in his 60s, he had returned and supported his limited monetary needs largely through hunting mountain lions and trapping otter. In 1921, after the Conyers moved back

Dave Lewis (on right) during a visit to Conyers' ranch on Cabin Creek around 1910. In the center is Edward Hanmer and on the left is Charlie Meyers. Hanmer was a miner, accomplished photographer, and brother of the doctor/ surgeon in the nearby gold mining boom town of Roosevelt, Idaho. Meyers was an early pioneer in the Middle Fork and South Fork areas and formerly had operated a horse-packing business between Warren and the gold diggings on Thunder Mountain. He probably was living on Cave Creek at the time of the photograph. Photograph from the Hanmer Collection Idaho State Historical Society (ISHS #P1994.25.1).

to Cabin Creek, Lewis applied (August 22) for a 62 acre homestead on the Trail Creek and adjacent properties. In his filing, he listed a three-room house (now called the "Dave Lewis cabin"), which probably had previously been occupied by the Conyers, and a small cabin, where he likely had formerly lived. By April 1922 Lewis' listing had been expanded to include an additional room on the now 14' x 32' house, a store house, and a cable car over Big Creek. He also had 12 head of horses and was raising timothy and clover hay for them and potatoes, onions, and other garden vegetables for himself. The 1918 Idaho National Forest inventory of livestock and agricultural lands indicates that Lewis had only 5 acres under cultivation and only a few more (15 total) horses at the time. There is no indication that he ever raised cattle.

The Homesteaders

T he Homestead Act of 1862 provided that the head of a family or anyone 21 years of age or older could file a claim on 160 acres of designated federal land for a fee of $14 at the time of filing and another $4 upon proof they had resided on the land for 5 years and plowed at least 10 acres into crops. The homesteader had to be on the land and start improvements within 6 months of filing. The 160 acres was largely based on conditions east of the Mississippi River Valley, where average annual precipitation was greater than 20 inches and generally accompanied by moderate temperatures and long growing seasons. In the arid portion of the country further west, where growing conditions were much harsher, 320 acres or much more proved to be necessary to sustain a family. Eventually the regulations were changed to reflect that fact but too late to affect the residents of Cabin Creek or elsewhere on Big Creek.

The stipulation that the land already be officially surveyed was a critical one. Federally sanctioned surveys in difficult to access and map mountainous or canyon lands generally were not done, especially if the area lacked substantial amounts of prime low-lying land along rivers or were not relatively easy to provide with water by irrigation. This was the situation for the expanse of land lying in the center of Idaho, extending west from the Salmon River to the eastern edge of the Payette River Valley and including Big Creek Country. In particular, Cabin Creek was not officially surveyed until 1908 and by that time it had been set aside under the Forest Reserve Act.

In 1891 Congress passed the General Revision Act that was designed to revise the nation's land laws. The act included a rider that allowed the President to establish "forest reserves." These were lands where human use and development, including homesteading, timber cutting, livestock grazing, and hunting, were prohibited. Two reserves were set aside in 1891, one in Wyoming and another in Colorado. In 1892, President Cleveland authorized the setting aside of more reserves but he refused to say where those would be until Congress passed legislation that provided means to enforce the prohibitions and manage the reserves. In 1897 Congress passed the Organic Act that placed the Forest Reserves under the Department of Interior to develop regulations for their use and management. The Department of Interior began assessment of the reserves in 1897 through its branch of the US Geological Survey. The Transfer Act of 1905 moved responsibility for the forest reserves to the Department of Agriculture under the newly established US Forest Service. Congress passed the Forest Reserves Homestead Act in 1906. In 1907, the forest reserves were changed to the status of national forests. The Idaho Reserve was established in 1908 and Cabin Creek was officially surveyed that October. A few years later in-holders were allowed to file homestead claims.

Under the Forest Reserves Homestead Act, the original Caswell Ranch on Cabin Creek eventually was subdivided into four parcels between 1910 and 1925, each meeting the 160-acre upper limit set by the federal government for homesteads at that time. As a result, three other names besides John Conyers' became prominent during this period: Orlando Mel Abel, his sister Sarah Elizabeth Bellingham, and Archie C. Bacon. As Abel's initial partner, John Routson also played a brief but critical role prior to the eligibility of the land for homesteading. Although the Cabin Creek area was deemed to be large enough to be divided into four separate homesteads under the original Homestead Act, in reality it prospered only when it was managed as one ranch and even then only when supplemented by use of adjacent grazing and forest lands and outside income. Nevertheless, if a person or family were to choose the one place to try to make a sustainable living off the land on 160 acres in the formidable Big Creek Country, it would be here.

ROUTSON–ABEL 1910–1911

The Routson–Abel occupancy of Cabin Creek represents a transition from squatter to homesteader. It also illustrates some of the difficulties that can arise during such a shift.

John Routson was a big man and all muscle. He stood 6 foot 2 inches and weighed about 190 pounds, at a time when most men were about 6 inches shorter and 25 pounds lighter. His ability and endurance on snowshoes were especially well known. John was a stock dealer on a rented farm in Weiser, Idaho before coming to the Big Creek area to live. He "discovered" the old Caswell place in the winter of 1909-1910 while on a snowshoeing expedition with a friend. His primary motivation probably was to trap for furs but he also had gone into the Big Creek/Chamberlain Basin country on a "scouting trip" after he had heard of possibilities for stock ranching in the area. He was looking for a place where he could raise a few horses and cows, maintain his wife and their five children, and do some prospecting. When Routson saw the ranch, he was immediately excited by its potential. In addition to having a house, numerous outbuildings, and a corral, it was well-equipped with farm machinery, pack saddles, and many other items. John was short of cash but he thought of a man named Mel Abel he had met in Resort [Warm Springs/Burgdorf], Idaho two years earlier who might be interested in going in with him on the purchase.

Mel Abel had been a railroad conductor in Washington state before moving to Idaho shortly after the turn of the century to take up farming. After Routson had spent the winter "looking up the proposition" [i.e., finding a suitable ranch site], he contacted Abel and they agreed to go into partnership. At the time, Routson was about 36 and Abel twelve years his senior. John returned to his family in Weiser in March and, with his 8-year old son John Jr. and Abel, left for the Big Creek ranch to take possession in April. They completed purchase of the place in May.

Abel and Routson bought Conyers' squatters' right, for which they probably received a quit claim deed, and the improvements, for which they may have received a separate bill of sale. The improvements included farming implements, the principal part of Conyers' cattle and horses, 5 or 6 small buildings, and fencing. The majority of the equipment and all of the buildings were left over from the Caswells. Abel paid out $2700 in cash and Routson contributed another $500 plus four head of horses and Abel carried Routson's note

Remains of the "milk house" near the mouth of Spring Creek in 1982. This building apparently provided temporary housing for John Routson and later Mel Abel during the period when they first occupied the former Caswell/ Conyer ranch. Photograph courtesy of the Payette National Forest.

for $850. At that time they did not think that the land was open to entry for homesteading. After taking possession of the place, John and his oldest son went out and brought in his 32 year old wife Lettie and his other children Adelia, Edna, Emmit, and Noel, ranging in age from eleven to one.

The partnership didn't last long. Abel and the Routson family lived together in the "old" Caswell cabin on Spring Creek through the summer of 1910 for a total of about 5 months — from May until November. During the winter of 1910-1911, Abel moved into the "milk house" about 50 feet southeast of the old home building because he and Routson could not get along and he wanted to be by himself. Also, as Abel later testified, "Mr. Routsen expected I was going to pay one half of the expenses of his family of seven and I did not think I could do it." In July, Abel moved into a tent about 1/4 mile below the Routsons on Cabin Creek, 30 feet from where the 1895 Caswell cabin had been located.

Sometime during the spring or summer of 1911, Abel learned that the land was open for entry but did not tell Routson. Also, during that time Abel and Routson got into an argument over ownership of the land. Now Routson moved into the old milk house and then went out for supplies and to determine who actually owned the land. Abel testified at a hearing on his homestead application in 1915, "Mr. Routsen and I had had a little quarrel and he said he was going out to see whether he owned the land or I owned it. And I went to Boise and learned [confirmed] that the land was open for entry and I went to Hailey and filed [on September 14, 1911]." Abel filed on 160 acres, or half of the patentable land in Section 25. It was the better of the two halves in having the most irrigated land, most of the cultivated hay land, and better access to the meadow but it did not include most of the original buildings, including the old Caswell home place. Some time after Routson returned, he learned that Abel had filed on the land. The two men argued again and Routson felt that Abel had not "done right by him." Abel stated that Routson . . . "wanted to sell out and walked away calling me inbred sons of bitches and such."

Their split created an animosity between the two that would plague Abel to his grave. Routson was hurt and angered by the action, especially since he had been the one to find the ranch in the first place and, rather than file on the remaining 160 acres, chose to sever the relationship he had with Abel. He and his family moved out and subsequently sold their portion in October 1911. They went to Edwardsburg for the winter, during which time the cabin they were living in there burned down and they lost most of their belongings. In the spring they moved to the former Yardley Ranch on Acorn Creek, which had 20-30 acres of tillable land amid otherwise rocky hillslope and forest. Prior to that, George Yardley had lived there as a bachelor farmer for about 5 years.

Routson's dislike for Abel and the way that he had been treated continued to fester for a long time. He protested Abel's homestead filing with the Government, was the cause of holding the patent up in subsequent proceedings, and apparently told a number of people that he would do everything he could to get Abel's homestead application cancelled.

After Routson moved to Acorn Creek, he continued to eke out a living for himself and his large family for another eight years. In 1915, according to the Idaho Statesman (April 3,1961), John was placer mining on Thunder Mountain but had a few cattle (the 1918 Idaho National Forest inventory lists 15) and horses (4) and a house on Acorn Creek. He even took on the job of mail carrier, from Warren to the Clover "postoffice" at Arthur Garden's place, enabling him to earn extra cash and possibly coincidentally, allowing him to exert control over mail deliveries to Abel. However, in mid November 1918 all of the Routson family except John moved back to Weiser so the children could attend school, and only John stayed year 'round to placer mine, run the ranch, and deliver mail. In 1924 Routson traded his whiteface cattle to Clarence Scott for half interest in a placer mine on Smith Creek. About that same time [1925], he sold the ranch to Walt Estep, a bachelor who applied for a homestead patent and received it in May 1929. Estep, then 36, had formerly been a forest ranger on the Paddy Flat District east of McCall (1921-1923) but gave it up to go mining on Ramey Ridge and farm on Acorn Creek.

ABEL-BACON 1911-1919

SOON AFTER his breakup with Routson, Abel contacted Archie Bacon and asked him to go into partnership. Bacon formerly had been a railroad engineer, which probably is how he and Abel had become acquainted, and wanted to try his hand at ranching. Both men were from Washington state, had known each other since about 1897, and were contemporary in age. Bacon put in $1,800 to buy Routson out. Initially, he apparently came to Cabin Creek on his own, leaving his wife Jennie and their two young daughters Ruth and Mary (ages 7 and 6, respectively) in Seattle. When Routson sold out on October 17, 1911, Abel and Bacon moved back up to the old home building from their temporary tent accommodations near the trail crossing. Bacon filed on the remaining 160 acres on November 10. In the winter of 1911-1912, Abel (with Bacon's help) built a new cabin for himself, about 40 feet southeast of the existing house, in order to be on his own claim. He moved there about the end of March. Bacon's family arrived in April 1912. Archie was 47 at the time and Jennie 5 years younger. For some unexplained reason, they

Abel's cabin on Spring Creek seen here in early 1920s. The cabin was Abel's "proving up" residence near the mouth of Spring Creek. At the time, it probably was occupied by Abel's three hired hands. One of Abel's hired men (Peter Gilstrap, far left) and three of the men (Dan Drake, Claude (Clay) Jordan, Glenn Morris) who had come in to retrieve Abel's body are shown. Photograph courtesy of the Idaho State Historical Society (ISHS #66-74.67 Earl Willson Collection).

decided to abandon the 1898 Caswell cabin. They set up a tent by the trail crossing and lived there until the weather turned cold in the fall when they moved in with Abel. In the spring, they built a three-room 21 x 25 foot log cabin on the former 1895 Caswell cabin site.

In his original application, Bacon had mistakenly claimed the west half of the northwest quarter of section 25 as part of his entry. This actually was uncultivatable hillside on Vinegar Hill. He had intended to claim the east half of the northwest quarter instead, which contained the old Caswell cabin and most of the other buildings plus some cultivatable land. He filed the Application for Amendment during 1913 and it was granted February 21, 1914. Bacon "made final proof" on his homestead on October 8, 1917, as witnessed by John Routson and David Lewis, and a final certificate was issued on October 20. By then he had added a separate 14 x 16 foot log store room, an 8 x 10 log poultry house, and an 8 x 10 underground cellar. During the two and a half years Abel and Bacon were partners, they ran 150-200 head of cattle at a time on the ranch and annually drove some of them the 125 miles over Elk Creek summit and through Warren to market in New Meadows. However, in July 1914 Bacon had a contract drawn up to dissolve their partnership because he and Abel were not getting along. A few years after the split, in 1918, Bacon was recorded as having 12 acres of his own under cultivation, 42 head of cattle, and 5 horses.

In October 1914, Charles L. Smith made application to contest Abel's homestead entry charging that, because of what he claimed was an error in locating the north-south property boundary, Abel had not resided on the land the proper length of time and had not culti-vated the required amount of land. As a result of Smith's action, the Government Land Office formally contested the entry on December 10, 1914. A formal hearing on Smith's challenge was held June 23, 1915 in Crawford, Idaho (a small town near present day Cascade later in-undated by the filling of Cascade Reservoir). Both sides were rep-resented by legal counsel. Smith was not present but A. C. Bacon, Arthur E. Garden, John W. Routson, and Harry McAdams testified as witnesses for Smith and George Yardley and Loula and Albert A. Kurry appeared as witnesses for Abel. John Conyers had been sub-poenaed to testify for Smith but claimed he was unable to attend be-cause of poor health. Abel also testified in his own behalf. Yardley had stayed with Abel a number of times, made his home there part of the time, and worked there. The Kurrys had camped at Abel's in the summers of 1912 and 1913 on the way to their new ranch at the mouth of Brush Creek on the Middle Fork and stayed with Abel all winter from about November 1913 to mid-April 1914.

Testimony was recorded in shorthand at the hearing with the un-derstanding that Smith would pay the cost of having it transcribed. During the testimony it came out that Smith had been a former employee of Bacon. In retrospect, it appears that Smith actually was acting in Routson's behalf. Also, Garden had been intimidated by Routson, who threatened to have him sent to the penitentiary for acting as a witness on Abel's homestead application and Garden held a grudge against Abel for allegedly misleading him about the information given on the application (although this was shown during the hearing not to be true). Both Yardley and Kurry testified that there was, as Abel's attorney put it, "... bad blood between Mr. Routsen, Mr. Garten [sic], and Mr. Bacon on one side and Mr. Abel on the other." The Kurrys testified that when they stayed overnight with the Routsons in the summer of 1914, John Routson told Loula Kurry that Abel had not treated him right and "I expect to do all I can to keep him from getting his homestead." Routson clearly continued to harbor that feeling at the time of the June 1915 hearing.

Action on the application dragged on for almost two more years on a variety of technicalities including the absence of a transcript of the hearing and intervention of the US Government into the proceedings. Because of Smith's failure to appear at the hearing and to pay the cost of the transcription, he eventually was eliminated from the case in June 1916. As intervener, the Government chose to pursue the contest which finally culminated in a decision to award the deed to Abel in May 1917 and Abel's patent finally was issued in January 1918. This pretty much dashed any hopes that Routson might have had about driving Abel from the land or acquiring the property for himself.

About two and a half years after Abel filed on his homestead, he got his sister Elizabeth Bellingham to file on another 160 acres to the north of him, in section 24, at the junction of Cabin and Cow Creeks. This provided additional range for grazing and assured access to timber and water. Apparently a small cabin, whose walls were four logs high and topped by frame construction sheathed with shakes, was erected on the property for Bellingham to live in. She probably lived there during the proving up period when she came to visit during the summer and possibly help her brother. The remainder of the time, Abel probably looked after their two homesteads and cattle and occupied the cabin. However, her patent was awarded on August 20, 1919 and after that time she would not have been required to live there in order to legally maintain ownership. At some point prior to that time, Abel's cabin near Spring Creek began to be used to house hired hands and possibly also occasional visitors. The 1918 Idaho National Forest inventory listed Abel and Bellingham together as having 70 head of cattle and 6 horses with Abel having 10 and Bellingham as having 20 acres in cultivation.

JAMES-HOMSLEY 1919-1920

Ed James, a re-current resident of Big Creek Country and Cabin Creek starting in the mid 1910s. Photograph by Bob Dustman in about 1950.

THE BACONS continued to homestead their portion until the spring of 1919, when an opportunity arose for them to leave the isolation of the mountains, enabling their daughters to go to school. Their adventure in wilderness living ended, the elder Bacons headed for Seattle and civilization with their now early-teenagers. The opportunity for them to leave was in the form of Ed James a young returning serviceman, who before the war had expressed the desire to take over the Bacon's ranch and cattle when he got back. Ed James first had come to Big Creek Country in 1916, trailing 50 head of cattle for Arthur ("Kid") and Viola Garden to their ranch on Garden Creek. At the time, the Clover post-office also was located there and Viola was the postmistress. Later Ed worked for Viola's nephew Joe Elliott on his ranch (at the head of Garden Creek eventually called Mile High) and lived in a small cabin he shared with Myron McCoy on Cave Creek about two miles up from where it entered Big Creek. Kid Garden died of influenza in the fall of 1918, while Ed was away during World War I, and the Garden Ranch was taken over by Joe Elliott and his brother Roy.

Soon after the start of the war, Ed volunteered for the army and was stationed for a little over a year in France. Early-on he was dosed with mustard gas and served the rest of the time behind the lines, which included taking care of horses. He returned to the United States in February 1919 and by early spring was on his way back into Big Creek country. After the snow on Elk Summit receded, Ed helped the Bacons go out, then met his wife Louise in McCall and headed back into Cabin Creek. It is possible that the Bacons or John Routson alerted Ed to potential problems with his future

Garden Creek basin and surrounding area as viewed from the south. The delta-shaped alluvial fan at the base of the basin was the location of the Archie and Viola Garden ranch and one site of the Clover postoffice. Their homestead included the wide bar along the southern shore of Big Creek and opposite the delta, which originally was the site of Wes Ritchey's cabin and later John Vines' cabin and landing strip. The knob about 3/4ths of the way up on the left is the approximate location of the Elliott/Cox ranch on Mile High. Photograph by Richard H. Holm Jr. October 2012.

neighbor Mel Abel, who they disparagingly referred to as "Baldy." While James was in France he had gotten acquainted with another young soldier named Gabe Homsley (age 22) and they had agreed to go in as partners on the ranch. Once Ed and Louise got settled at the Bacon place, he sent for Gabe. That summer, Gabe also went out and got his wife Mildred and they moved into Ed's old place on Cave Creek.

A PERIOD OF UPHEAVAL 1919-1920

IN A MERE moment in time in the history of Cabin Creek, between spring 1919 and autumn 1920, major changes in occupancy and ownership came to pass. First, the Bacon family left after eight years of residence and toil, to be replaced by two new couples full of hope and dreams — Ed James and Gabe Homsley and their wives. While this sort of transition was relatively common among homesteaders, the next major event, the brutal murder of Mel Abel, was not. After Abel's death, his estate went to his sister Elizabeth Bellingham and, along with it, the responsibility for the management of their two homesteads and herd of purebred cattle. Elizabeth was not suited for the life of a rancher, especially in the wilds of Idaho, but neither was she a quitter. She also may have had a streak of stubbornness that caused her to resolve that whoever had killed her brother would not benefit further from it. Elizabeth was fortunate to be able to persuade John Conyers and his wife to return to Cabin Creek, after an absence of ten years, to manage the combined Abel-Bellingham ranch for her. The arrangement probably included some share of the cattle produced from her herd and provided for the incorporation or disposition of any cattle he had been raising at Trail Creek. Amidst this shuffling of faces were added the abrupt departures of the Homsley and James families and of Abel's hired hands.

The winter of 1919-1920 was a great one for trapping. An article in the January 2, 1920 Payette Lake Star, a McCall, Idaho newspaper, reported that "John Routson is killing two birds this winter while carrying mail to Clover. He has a line of traps along the route." In March, the Star ran a photograph of John with Jake Jensen [Janson]

*Bellingham cabin (right) and storage annex (left) where Mel Abel was resid-
ing at the time of his death. Men are four of those who had been sent in from
Cascade to retrieve Abel's body; they also were accompanied by A. C. Behne,
the postmaster of Yellow Pine, who gathered the census during the trip. View
is facing south. Photograph courtesy of the Payette National Forest.*

showing some of their catch of furs and noting that "John Routson
will total around $1,000 and many others have made better than
wages trapping."

On the other hand, it was a rough winter for ranching. The
Garden Ranch lost all of their cattle, the Abel Ranch lost 70-
80%, and James and Homsley lost 50%. Ed James claimed that
the reason he and Gabe were able to save half their herd was
because they had more hay and put the cattle on the steep moun-
tainsides to graze, where the snow was thinner. However, it also
is possible that Abel's herd lacked proper oversight or was extensively pirated during this time.

Abel's misfortune that winter extended beyond just his cattle.
On the evening of December 15, 1919, he went to feed the cattle
from a hay stack near where Calf Creek joins Cabin Creek. Peter
Gilstrap (age 74) and G. O. McDermand (age 47) were working for
him at the time. They apparently were staying in Abel's cabin on
Spring Creek and Abel was occupying his sister's cabin at the mouth
of Cow Creek. McDermand had just hired on the previous month.
When Abel did not come for dinner, McDermand reportedly went
to look for him and found the cattle all around the stack and Abel

lying in their midst. Ed James later recounted in his autobiography that after "...McDerrmat [sic] found Baldy dead, [he] came and got me.... So I was the second person to see him dead. The authorities questioned me, also Joe Elliot, who was known to have words with Baldy." Remarkably, McDermand, Gilstrap, and another man Erick Johnson [or was this actually Jake Janson's brother?] did not write to notify the county coroner of Abel's death until December 27 and, though postmarked at Clover the next day, the letter was not received until January 8. The letter requested the coroner "to come to the accident" to retrieve the body which was "supposed to be killed by a bull" and not yet buried though kept frozen in the snow.

On January 9, 1920 the Payette Lake Star reported that Abel's "death is said to have resulted from the attack of an enraged bull on December 15. This is the story as was told to J. W. Routson, who carries the mail from Warren to Clover, and brought by him to Warren on his last trip out." Further on in the article it was noted "It was known that he [Abel] had enemies, and it is said that his life had been threatened. Suspicions of foul play are strengthened by the fact that news of the tragedy was not given out until two weeks after the body is said to have been discovered." Mel Abel apparently was the kind of person one either liked a lot or hated; there was no middle ground. It is not hard to conceive that someone might explode in anger or harbor a hatred with sufficient intensity to murder him. Also that person might find support for the deed, either in cooperative action or silence.

Four experienced mountaineers were hired to retrieve the body because almost all of the route was over rough terrain in deep snow. They didn't leave until about 12 days after news of Abel's murder reached the outside. It took them another 19 days by skis and snowshoes to reach the scene and tow the body on a toboggan back to Scott Valley a few miles east of Cascade, about 260 miles round trip. One of the men Dan Drake was sworn in as deputy coroner. The other three, Clay Jordan, Glenn Morris, and John Williams, were former servicemen. The group was met in Yellow Pine on their way in and accompanied the rest of the way by the postmaster and official census taker A. C. Behne.

Site of Mel Abel's murder. View is easterly about midway along the present-day landing strip. Photograph courtesy of the Payette National Forest.

Behne used the opportunity to complete his official census of Big Creek residents. When they arrived at Abel's cabin, Gilstrap and McDermand were still there looking after the place and taking care of the stock. The recovery team spent several days at Cabin Creek, where they examined and photographed the murder scene and wrapped the frozen body in several layers of cloth and freshly killed deer hides before leaving. They also obtained a hay knife from near the scene of Abel's death that reportedly ". . . still had

Body of Mel Abel on its way from Cabin Creek to Cascade. Photograph courtesy of the Idaho State Historical Society (ISHS #66-74.257 Earl Willson Collection).

telltale evidence clinging to the blade" and also collected the head of the bull which was purported to have been the cause of death.

Gabe Homsley accompanied the men on the return trip. Ed James didn't go out with them, even though he had been the second one on the scene, probably because his wife was about to give birth. Homsley may have wanted to accompany the group in order obtain some supplies and to file a homestead application, which he submitted on February 5, 1920 just a few days after the body arrived in Cascade. The application was for an unclaimed parcel on Cabin Creek, located between the Abel and Bellingham homesteads. It was much closer to the land he and Ed were leasing and to the Jamses' cabin than was his Cave Creek residence.

On January 30, 1920 the Cascade News noted "The body showed gruesome evidences of the tragedy that resulted in Mr. Abel's death, such as frightful wounds of the head, a broken arm and leg, and other marks of the encounter." The article also inferred that the death had resulted from an encounter with a bull. However, in its February 6, 1920 issue, the Payette Lake Star reprinted the January 30 Cascade News article in full but raised serious question as to the cause of death stating "In fact, if that article so worded, had appeared in this paper you could bet your last dollar that it was dodging the issue. The people up in this neck of the woods can understand plain language, and they want the conclusion of those who made the investigation as to what caused the death of O. M. Abel."

Abel's sister was waiting in Cascade, along with an undertaker from Walla Walla, to prepare the body for shipment. Abel had been a 32nd degree Mason and his Masonic Lodge arranged for the undertaker and retrieval of the body from Cabin Creek and shipment to Walla Walla. However, the body was first taken to Nampa, Idaho for autopsy. An article with a Nampa dateline published in the Cascade News on February 20 stated that "the information given the authorities convinces them that murder was committed, instead of killing by the animal suspected." "Investigation shows that death was caused by a narrow, blunt instrument, with which Mr. Abel had been struck three times over the forehead and one blow over the ear had pierced the skull. A hayknife found near where the body was first discovered was believed to have been the weapon used and it exactly corresponds with the indentations on the victim's skull."

No one was ever convicted of the murder, presumably because of the lack of witnesses and the absence of any confession. In March 1920, McDermand was brought out from Cabin Creek, under the guise of serving as a witness, but actually to be arrested for the murder. However, he was released about three weeks later presumably because, as the Cacade News (April 9, 1920) reported, "the circumstantial evidence in the possession of the prosecuting attorney was considered insufficient to warrant a trial of the case."

McDermand told the newspaper that he planned to return to the ranch and remain there until the snow receded enough that he could bring his horse out. Later, he allegedly left the country with some of Abel's possessions, possibly because he believed he was due them in place of unpaid wages. Apparently Bacon was not directly involved because he and his family had already gone out of the area the previous spring. Though none of the newspaper articles at the time of Abel's death mentioned either James or Homsley as possible suspects, neither man is beyond suspicion since a harsh winter and impending loss of their cattle could have caused them to break under the stress. Also, James, like his friend Routson, maintained that a bull had killed Abel and one could have been providing an alibi for the other. Surprisingly, no one seems to have implicated John Routson even though he had an established motive and his mail deliveries brought him regularly into the vicinity of Abel's ranch. Interestingly, it was Routson who told the Payette Lakes Star that Abel had been gored, potentially further throwing off any chance of suspicion.

Gabe Homsley and his wife stayed a while longer but Mildred didn't like it there so he went back with her to North Dakota. He was killed soon after in a horse riding accident but not before Mildred conceived two daughters. Ed's wife Louise delivered their first child (Althea) at the ranch on March 6, 1920, with only Ed to help. That summer, Ed had to put up the hay alone. Eventually, the Jameses moved to Acorn Creek to put up John Routson's hay. Ed stayed and fed John's cattle that winter (1920-1921) and sometimes took his place carrying mail. The following summer, the Jameses' second child (Ethel) was born (August 13, 1921) at Acorn Creek. Ed delivered her also but May Conyers came up afterward from Cabin Creek to help out for a few days. Louise was not in good health, so she and Ed decided to get out of the back country. He traded for an old buckboard and harness and eventually made it to Fall River Mills, California, where his older brother and sister and her husband lived. But over 20 years later, he would return to Big Creek Country and to Cabin Creek.

CONYERS 1920-1925

APPARENTLY, ELIZABETH BELLINGHAM contacted John Conyers, now age 60, by mail at his Trail Creek residence soon after her brother Abel's death and arranged for him to manage the Bellingham and Abel ranches at Cabin Creek. This was a wicked twist of fate since Conyers, who was the original cause of the boundary dispute over the location of Abel's homestead residence, indirectly had sided with Routson and Bacon and opposed Abel during the preliminary hearings. As it would turn out, Conyers was wrong about his interpretation of where the boundary between the two properties actually ran and Abel was closer to being correct. Presumably old Gilstrap was the only one left to take care of the Abel/Bellingham cattle and watch over their belongings until the Conyers arrived.

John and May probably got there by late spring or early summer 1920. They apparently re-occupied the old Caswell ranch house and re-established the house garden. In addition to the combined Abel/Bellingham properties and other unclaimed land, Conyers probably utilized the Bacons' pasture and hay fields, which were unoccupied after Ed James left. Conyers ran about 220 head of cattle, of which 160 may have been Bellingham's and the rest his own. The interpersonal, sociological, and economic drama played out over the better part of the previous decade ultimately conspired to (temporarily at least) reconnect and repair linkages with the landscape that had been artificially severed when the Cabin Creek land had been broken up into small homesteads.

Between the Abel and Bellingham portions on Cabin Creek there was an unoccupied 40-acre quarter section and, while he was managing the ranch for Bellingham, Conyers filed on it in May 1921. However, the Land Office discovered that it was the same parcel that Gabe Homsley had filed on the previous year and had priority, so Conyers' application was returned. The Forest Service inspected the land and recommended that it be expanded to 95 acres to include the remaining adjacent cultivatable land on the east and west sides of Cabin Creek, to avoid isolating parcels of National Forest Lands. By the time of Conyers' application, Homsley and his wife had left the country for Fairfield, North Dakota and Conyers had to obtain Homsley's formal withdrawal of his application before he could re-apply. When Conyers resubmitted his request, he expanded it to 140 acres. This tract included the 95 acres identified in the Forest Service survey (and was identical to the tract later obtained by Merl and Jean Wallace). The District Forest Office did not receive a satisfactory release from Homsley until the end of 1921. On May 25, 1922, Conyers received a letter from the Acting District Ranger notifying him that the tract had been listed with the Secretary of the Interior and informing him that "You will not, however, be able to file on it until it has been restored to entry by the Interior Department. The Supervisor may, however, be willing to issue you a special use permit to occupy and improve it until such time as entry can be made. You will receive a letter by registered mail from the Land Office at Hailey, Idaho, informing you of the date on which filing will be accepted and that you have a preference right of 60 days within which to make entry and you should see to it that your entry is made within this period." Apparently that date would finally arrive in 1924.

At the time of Conyers application for his own homestead in May 1921, there were no improvements present. Normally he and his wife would have built a cabin on the new property and occupied it in order to "prove up" on the homestead. However, since they did not receive official authorization to file until 1924, they apparently did not do this and continued to live at the old Caswell place. But, they probably used the additional property for grazing cattle and raising crops even before they could file on it. In fact, they may never have built a cabin there because in September 1925 Bellingham sold her last 160 head of cattle to Tom Carrey, who lived along the South Fork, and no longer needed Conyers' services. It is not known if the Conyers stayed around after that but there may have been little incentive for them to do so.

At this point Idaho and the nation were in an economic slump which would only worsen. The Conyers may have remained a while longer in the Big Creek basin at Edwardsburg but eventually they made their way to near Middleton (Marble Front School area), Canyon County, Idaho, where they rented a place and farmed until John's death in 1938. The departure of the Conyers marked the beginnings of a shift in land use from cattle ranching to dude ranching.

Artificial boundaries and thoughtlessly imposed size limits, effectively fragmented the landscape and severed the ecological interconnections that had enabled the Caswells to sustain themselves. These constraints set arbitrarily and with inadequate knowledge of climate, geology, and topography were unrelated to the proper functioning and operation of a productive and reasonably self-sustaining ranch ecosystem. Imposition of inadequate size limits for self-sufficiency in the region and artificial boundaries in this arid and discontinuous landscape severely hampered the homesteaders' chances for success.

⤙ The Hard Timers ⤚

(Pre- and Post-WWII Depression Era)

Farmers and ranchers in Idaho struggled economically for many years through a financial downturn that started shortly after the first World War and went into free-fall in the autumn of 1929 at the start of the nation's Great Depression. Those who followed the original Cabin Creek homesteaders were severely constrained by inadequate funds and an inability to turn a profit because of depressed cattle prices, limited hay production, difficult access, and the long distance to markets. In spite of their hard work and creativity, the would-be residents of Cabin Creek during this period, which encompassed not only the Great Depression but also World War II, were destined to struggle just to hold on and keep from going under financially. Most of them did not succeed.

BELLINGHAM AND SUCCESSORS 1925-1956

ELIZABETH BELLINGHAM MANAGED to hang on to the combined Bellingham and Abel homesteads for an additional 27 years after her brother's murder until her own death in 1947. Little is known about what happened on the two homesteads during the remaining time after she sold her cattle herd in the autumn of 1925. She did continue to visit Cabin Creek periodically during the summer, including in 1933, to check on her ranch. Those who lived there and tried to squeeze out a living did so only temporarily and rarely did more than break even. The property may have remained idle between 1925 and 1930. After that she may have struck a deal, involving the land and her horses, with Merl Wallace after he and his wife occupied the adjacent lands in 1931 (see next section). However, she apparently could be as disagreeable as her brother and that arrangement, if it ever existed, ended by May 1934 when she wrote Dave Lewis looking for someone who would take care of her place. In his April 16,

Bellingham's cabin as it looked in 1982. East (doorway) and north sides are shown, south side was covered by hop vines. Photograph courtesy of the Payette National Forest.

1934 letter to Jean, Merl noted that a man named "Wy" was living in the Bellingham homestead cabin. "Wy has had a lot of visitors this spring. The Goldmans, Richard's daughter from the Golden Hand [Mine] and Emmet Routsons' wife." Some of the people he mentioned in April were still living there at the time of his November 28 letter to Jean. He indicated that Mrs. Gildner was very ill and that Mrs. Goldman had been doing triple duty as doctor, nurse, and cook. In the spring of 1935 Jess Warner (aka Vanderpool) and his wife Vernie leased the Bellingham-Abel ranch and moved there with the rest of their family (Vernie's daughters Aloha and Lila Beck and their two-year old stepbrother Jess Jr.).

The Warners had been living at the Monumental Creek Ranch but,

Jess (Vanderpool) Warner. Photo by Joe Bayok.

Cabin built for the Warner family on the Bellingham homestead in the mid 1930s. Photograph by Joe Bayok.

when they couldn't make the payments, turned it back to the seller Roy Elliott and two years later ended up at Cabin Creek. Jess' last name was really Vanderpool but he was wanted for horse stealing, so when in the Yellow Pine-Big Creek area he went by the name of Warner. The Warners spent the first year in the homestead cabin that appeared to a visitor Joe Bayok to be two wall tents that had a breezeway between them and with a roof over the whole thing. In the spring of 1936, at Vernie's request, Joe, Guy Baker, and Howard Elkins built a two-story cabin to provide more suitable accommodations. The building was completed in about two weeks, from logs salvaged from one of the other homesteads and new ones they cut out of the forest. They were still living at Cabin Creek in June when Dave Lewis came by on his way out of Big Creek to seek medical attention. When he left, Aloha followed him at a distance to make sure he made it safely to the next stop at Acorn Creek. Dave eventually rode all the way to Edwardsburg where an ambulance was summoned but, a short time later, he died at the Veteran's Hospital in Boise.

Myron "Skook" McCoy (front) and Aloha (Beck) McCoy in the early 1930s. Photograph by Joe Bayok.

In the summer of 1936, Jess went to work packing for a surveying crew and Aloha took a job at the hotel in Big Creek Village, which was run by Dick Cowman. In mid-September, Vernie brought baby Jess for Aloha to tend; when Aloha refused because of her job, Vernie went ballistic and started screaming at her. Both Jess and Aloha's boy friend Myron "Skook" McCoy (age 21) heard about it and "everyone" decided that the 16-year old Aloha and Skook should get married right away for her protection. Myron and Aloha McCoy later lived two winters at Cabin Creek. After that, a parade of other people occupied the Bellingham/Abel Ranch. Some leased from Mrs. Bellingham, others just moved in. Starting in the spring of 1938, the Thompsons were there for a while, followed by Myron's brother Les and his wife Thelma.

From 1938-1940, Les and Thelma and their young daughter Pat lived in the 2-story cabin. Among other things, Les managed the cattle for Blackie Wallace, packed dudes, and delivered the U.S. mail. The family often exchanged visits with the newly wed Lafe and Emma Cox, who lived 6 miles away on an exposed mountain-top ranch they called Mile High. According to the Coxes, the name came from the fact there was a mile of telephone line between their cabin and the old Garden homestead on Big Creek, which they referred to by its post office name of Clover. However, the location where the ranch house was situated also was just over a mile high (5480 feet).

The Mile High ranch had formerly belonged to the Elliott brothers. Originally there were four: Joe, Roy, Ernest ("Hardrock"), and Bert, who were nephews of Viola Garden and who ran cattle and put up hay there. After Kid Garden died and Viola moved away, the brothers gave up ranching but Joe proved up on the homestead in January 1920. Bert was killed in 1926 near Elk Summit when struck in the head by a rock, which apparently had come from dynamiting by a road crew working nearby. The other brothers gradually drifted away until only Ernest was left. He reportedly contracted spotted fever and died there in May 1934. Vernie Warner, one of her daughters, and two Forest Service employees were helping to care for him at the time. Lafe bought the place in Fall

Joe and Carole Mabee at Cabin Creek in February 1947. Photographs by Bob Fogg provided by Richard H. Holm Jr.

1938 for $500 from a gambler he knew who was down on his luck and needed money. The Coxes built a hunting lodge and airstrip there. They sold the ranch to Bill Williams and settled outside of Yellow Pine. Williams sold it to the Idaho Fish and Game in 1949 for

$8,500; after that it was used as a winter game range and leased to an outfitter.

Joe Mabee was 42 when he showed up in the Cabin Creek area around 1945. Joe wanted to buy the Flying W Ranch from Jean Wallace. According to her, he even "moved in," but she didn't want to sell and leased it to Lafe Cox instead. Joe had grown up in the Boise Valley and worked several years with his father in the cattle business before striking off on his own to work as an oil driller in Oklahoma and a shipyard worker in California. He had two daughters by a previous marriage, Billy Jean and Genevieve, but they remained with their mother in Boise. He subsequently married Carole Brunholtz in 1942, when she was 22. The Mabees apparently began leasing the Bellingham-Abel ranch and formally began dude ranching in 1945. Elizabeth Bellingham was ill and knew little of what was going on in the back country but in April 1946 Joe and Carole were her house guests in Walla Walla. Carole may have been pregnant at the time or recently given birth to their first child Joe. After Elizabeth's death in September 1947, the Bellingham/Abel property went to her nephew, Edward M. Barnes. Within a short time the Mabees purchased the combined 320 acres from Barnes in December 1949 for $8000. They renamed it the Pinto Ranch, stocked it with 22 of their trademark pinto horses, and hired Ed James to wrangle dudes and guide hunters. James had come back into the area after living for a while in Klammath Falls, Oregon raising foxes. In his memoir Ed is recorded as saying "Carol was as wonderful a person as Joe was no good and that is saying a lot."

In 1951, Ed James' daughter Althea returned to her birth place on Cabin Creek and went on a three-week, 180-mile pack trip with him. At the time, she was a 31-year old school teacher from Aberdeen, Washington and they hadn't seen each other in many years. She flew from McCall on a Forest Service plane, so Ed may have been packing for the Forest Service that summer. They visited many of Ed's old haunts in the vicinity of Cold Meadows and McCalla Creek (Root Ranch). The next year (December 1952), Ed married Addie (Adalyne) Moore. Ed was 56 and Addie about 18. She had come to Big Creek in 1947 from Harney, Oregon with her father Dewey and older sister Virginia. The Moores settled on the old Routson/Estep/Beal place on Acorn Creek.

Prior to their arrival, the property had been occupied briefly by two other owners after Estep sold it to Phil Beal in 1932.

In the spring of 1951, the Mabees' second child Carolyn Jo was born. They left Cabin Creek in late March to be near a doctor and returned in mid-May. Virgina Moore came down from Acorn Creek to look after the ranch while they were away. That September the Mabees sold the Pinto Dude Ranch and stock to Gordon Ray of the Ray Petroleum Transportation Company and Arley E. White. However, the Mabees apparently remained on the ranch through the hunting season and did not leave until 1952. In 1953, they moved to Reno where Joe operated a construction business until his retirement to Klammath Falls, Oregon.

Ray and White continued to operate under the name of the Pinto Ranch, though White apparently did not participate in its actual operation. Ed James stayed on to work for Gordon Ray. Ed is quoted in his memoir as saying "All in all, there is a world full of worse fellows than Gordon, and he meant well, but if there ever was a dude, he was it." Ray bought White out three years later and lasted two more years before getting out himself, probably at the end of the 1956 hunting season. By that time, he had a string of 21 head of horses and mules that he grazed under permit on the National Forest from April through December. Six head were allowed to graze free under a ranch permit. The remainder were assessed under a packer permit at $1.20 per head per month for a total of $162. Ray would have had to provide hay for the stock the rest of the winter or trail them out of the backcountry.

It is possible that Ed James stayed around until Gordon Ray left. He and Addie left the backcountry while Ed was in his 60s. They later divorced and he ended up owning a ranch in Grants Pass, Oregon where he lived until he was 82. In December 1976, he left to be with his son in Costa Rica and died there in 1984.

Gordon Ray sold his ranch, including the pinto horses, to Loren K. Hollenbeak in 1956. Ray's leaving marked the end of the small-time, break-even or go-broke rancher and outfitter/guide operations on the Abel/Bellingham portion of Cabin Creek.

WALLACE 1930-1959

MERL "BLACKIE" WALLACE was a US Forest Service ranger for nine years in the 1920s. Initially he was with the Payette Forest in Emmett, Idaho but in April 1927 he transferred to the Idaho National Forest (later to become part of the Payette) in McCall. During the snow-covered period he worked in the office but the remainder of the year was spent patrolling parts of the forest. He and Jean Orr were married in May 1927 in Boise, Idaho. Through her's and her family's connections, they got the Republican Governor H. C. Baldridge to perform the ceremony. That summer and fall Merl and Jean were at the Paddy Flat Ranger Station southeast of McCall. But in 1929 Merl was assigned to the Cold Meadows Ranger Station, which Jean described in her unpublished autobiography as "the most remote and inaccessible of the three backcountry districts" in the Idaho Forest, the others being Chamberlain Basin District to the west of it and Big Creek District south of that. The lower half of the Big Creek river basin actually was part of the Cold Meadows District.

Merl Wallace. Photograph from the Wallace Special Collection, University of Idaho Library.

Dave Lewis, Thelma Page, and Merl Wallace at the memorial for Private Harry Eagan [Egan] on Soldier Bar in summer 1928. Photograph (MG190 #54) by Warren Bolles of the Cold Meadows Ranger District from Dave Lewis Special Collection (MS Accession #2011-03), University of Idaho Library.

Merl previously had been into the Big Creek area during at least three other years (1924, 1926, & 1928). He reportedly was the first ranger on the Cold Meadows District and in 1924-1925, with the aid of his fire control assistant Emmit Routson, built a bunkhouse and commissary there. In the summer of 1928, he and another Cold Meadows ranger Warren H. Bolles accompanied Dave Lewis and Thelma Page to Soldier Bar to visit the memorial to Private Eagan [Egan]. During that trip, they may have stopped at Cabin Creek (about 9 miles upriver) at what then was known as the "Conyers Ranch." Thelma grew up in Boise but recently had been employed by the War Department in Washington, DC, where the request for construction of the monument was first implemented, and she may have been visiting the site with the two Forest Rangers, in order to inspect it.

Jean Wallace in front of the Caswell 1898 cabin, which at this point had been moved to the Wallace homestead. Photograph from the Wallace Special Collection (MS Accession #2011-03), University of Idaho Library.

The monument had been erected only a few years earlier in the autumn of 1925 by Joe Elliott, under contract with the War Department, and with the help of Dave Lewis and Harry Shellworth. Shellworth was a friend of Dave's and a frequent visitor into Big Creek Country. At the time, Joe was the postmaster at the Clover post office near Garden Creek, a job he had assumed after his uncle died in 1918 and his aunt Viola Garden left the area.

The engraved headstone for the monument, which weighed over 200 pounds not including crating, had undergone an interesting journey prior to reaching Soldier Bar. After its preparation by the Vermont Marble Company, it was transported from their quarry in Proctor to the Quartermaster Depot in Boston for shipment by steamer to Portland, Oregon. From Portland, it went by train to McCall, Idaho where it was received by Elliott and transported nearly 90 miles by wagon to Edwardsburg, via Warren, and then 40 miles by mule to Soldier Bar!

Jean Wallace's introduction to the Big Creek region with Merl was quite an ordeal for her. She later recalled "On June 1, 1929 we set out to cross Elk Summit [on the old Warren — Big Creek Wagon Road], the party consisting of twenty men, the rangers of the [three backcountry] districts and their trail crews, [fire] guards and lookouts, some sixty head of horses and mules — and me the lone woman. We broke camp at Elk Creek at 4:00 A.M., and after battling snow and altitude on foot over Elk Summit all day I finally fell into the door of the Werdenhoff Mine at 7:00 P.M., was given a shot of illegal but medicinal whiskey, passed out and slept three days."

The rest of the crew went on without her but eventually were located by phone at the Big Creek Headquarters "... and soon Blackie and Jimmy Farrell, the Deputy Supervisor, rode over and collected me, and then began my never-to-be-forgotten first journey into the Big Creek Country clear around the Big Creek and Cold Meadows Districts, down to the main Salmon River at Disappointment, ... and back up Big Creek. It was June, and Oh, the wild flowers and the trees and the lakes and the streams and the wild animals I saw! It was during this journey I met the love of my life, the Big Creek Country, and found the ranch in the wilderness that afterward became my home. There at the place where Cabin Creek flows into Big Creek was the old [Caswell] Ranch ... and the wide meadows, the old houses, and the chuckling Cabin Creek and the whispering cottonwoods captivated me and made me know this was the place I could call home."

"We did not take it over for a while, first there was a year of duty at Cold Meadows during which I got to know the back country as few women have, traveled a week through the trailess wilderness to a fire on Two Point Peak [George & Skook McCoy and Ed James were there too, as packers for the Forest Service], met the famous cougar hunter 'Uncle Dave Lewis,' and his hounds, became friends with Mrs. Edwards of Edwardsburg and her husband and son, Napier, ran into hidden whiskey stills, met crazy men and bootleggers, trappers and miners, and was adopted by the Jansen [Janson] brothers, Jake [age 55] and Eric [59], two wonderful old Finns who had the Snowshoe Mine and the cabin on Crooked Creek, where they were hosts to all who passed by and friends and guardians to the whole Back Country population."

Although the Wallaces were able to acquire property on Cabin Creek, it initially was not the idyllic ranch they imagined when Jean had first seen the place. In fact, they had to settle for the least suitable of the original four homestead sites, one that John Conyers had filed on but never actually resided on. Eventually though, through a stroke of good fortune, they also were able to acquire the former Bacon homestead and bring their total holdings to 300 acres. However, they would always be plagued by the inability to acquire the strategically-placed Bellingham-Abel properties.

Jake (second from right) and Eric Janson (center) in the gateway of their home on Crooked Creek. Photograph courtesy of the Idaho State Historical Society (ISHS #66-74.64 Earl Willson Collection).

In November 1929, Merl telephoned S. C. Scribner the Forest Supervisor in McCall to inquire about ownership of the homestead between the Bellingham and the Bacon-Abel properties, which Conyers had filed on in December 1924. He received a written reply which indicated that Conyers had relinquished his claim in November 1925 and that later that month it had been filed on by Charles Hefner, who relinquished his claim in September 1926, and subsequently filed on by Ernest E. Elliott in March 1927. Ernest lived with his brother Joe on his nearby homestead at Mile High. Because Ernest had not filed on a homestead previously, he could legally file on this one. Ernest claimed Conyers had abandoned his application but subsequent events would indicate this was not so and that Hefner must have defaulted on his payment to Conyers.

In 1930, Merl resigned his job with the Forest Service and he and Jean took steps to acquire the Conyers homestead and first oc-cupied it in June although for official purposes Merl reckoned (when his homestead claim was inspected by Ranger Dan H. LeVan in July 1936) that actual residence was established July 1, 1931. After nego-tiations with Conyers and Ernest Elliott, the Wallaces filed a new entry on December 18, 1930 and their patent eventually was granted in April 1937. Initially they may have lived in the old Caswell home-place at the mouth of Spring Creek but they realized that they soon would have to move onto the former Conyers property to officially begin "proving up" on it. That winter, Merl got a man named Ed Applegate to caretake the place.

When the Wallaces began looking into acquiring a place on Cabin Creek, they apparently also inquired about the availability of the Bacon homestead. After the Jameses left the Bacon home-stead in 1921, it probably remained vacant for several years except for whatever use Conyers might have made of the pasture and hay fields and the former Caswell buildings. In 1928 the Bacons sold their homestead to James A. Kesgard and his wife for $500. The Kesgards had no interest in the property and made the deal with the Bacons solely for the benefit of their friend Douthitt who con-templated organizing a corporation. However, after the stock mar-ket crash in October 1929, Douthitt's plans probably changed and the Kesgards were never paid nor were the Bacons. On February 20, 1931 the Bacons filed a complaint to foreclose on the mortgage, claiming they were due $784.73 to cover the principal plus interest, taxes, and other expenses. The Kesgards defaulted on the judge-ment and the property was scheduled to be sold by the sheriff on August 25, 1931. All of these delays and legal maneuvers served to benefit Merl and Jean, who were looking to expand their holdings beyond what they had recently acquired from Conyers. Apparently, the Wallaces, through Jean's mother Annabelle Orr, struck a deal with the Kesgards for $840, three days before the public sale. A few years later, on August 27, 1934, they officially obtained the property from Annabelle.

The Wallaces returned to Cabin Creek in the spring of 1931, after Jean's job as an aide for the state legislature ended for the year and the road over Elk Summit opened. Earlier that year, the Forest Service had sent in a trail crew to extend the Big Creek trail from the Dave Lewis Ranch to the Middle Fork of the Salmon River. Because of an impassable gorge near the mouth of Big Creek, the existing trail took a circuitous route up Trail Creek (probably listed on maps as Pioneer Creek starting around the mid 1920s) from the Lewis ranch, then over Burnt Creek Summit, and down Brush Creek to reach the Middle Fork. The trail construction was part of the preparations for formal designation of the surrounding country as the Idaho Primitive Area. Primitive area status would emphasize historical-style recreational uses such as hiking, horse packing, and tent camping and restrict road construction and commercial logging.

On April 21, one of the Forest Service trail crew members John Reeder and Dave Lewis came into Cabin Creek to use the telephone to get help for another member who had been injured in the gorge by falling rock. Noel Routson, the youngest son of John Routson, had been partially buried by a cave-in about 10 that morning. He was unconscious for about 20 minutes and went into shock. Reeder probably had run to Lewis' ranch and, finding no telephone there, borrowed a horse from Lewis to ride to the nearest one at Cabin Creek and Dave had come along for company. It was decided to clear a field at Cabin Creek and land an airplane there while Noel was being transported on a stretcher the 12 miles up the Big Creek

Noel Routson (on litter) being readied for evacuation on first flight ever made from Cabin Creek. Photograph courtesy of the Payette National Forest.

trail from the gorge. A day later, Noel was successfully evacuated to a Boise hospital on the first flight ever made from Cabin Creek, with former World War I pilot Bill Gowan at the controls. The plane landed and took off on a bench on the Bellingham place northeast of the junction of Cabin and Cow Creeks.

Emphasis on the use of the Idaho Primitive Area for traditional forms of recreation, pushed the Wallaces to develop their place into a "guest ranch." Provision of outfitting and guide services would allow them to supplement their income from cattle ranching and Jean's work with the legislature. It didn't take them long to also realize that the presence of the landing field used to evacuate Noel Routson could facilitate the establishment of a guest ranch at Cabin Creek. The Wallaces hoped to capitalize on the availability of the landing site and abundant wildlife to develop the recreational aspects of hunting and fishing for paying clients. After a landing field was established adjacent to their property, they ran the combined Conyers-Bacon homesteads as the Flying W Ranch. Access from their property to the landing strip was through Bellingham property.

Merl continued to work on the ranch during the summer of 1931 to prepare it for occupation, and Jean apparently returned to Boise. Two helpers with the surname of Mason assisted Merl by herding horses out of the meadow hayfield and doing the irrigating. In a letter written in mid-June, Merl told Jean that he had been working on the "summer kitchen." "I am making a partition length wise giving the kitchen 8 feet and the dining room 10 ft. wide by 13 ft. long with three doors one on the north end, one on the south west corner and one in the south corner for the guests to enter. The walls are 6 ft. 9 inches high with four ft. walled up with shakes and two ft. nine in. [with] screen and we can get drop canvas later on and use the kitchen late in the fall." He also had set up two wall tents borrowed from the Janson brothers. One of them was torn across the ridge pole and the other had a lot of holes in it, so he asked Jean to bring some mending paste and canvas for making repairs. A few years later in May 1934 Merl moved the summer kitchen up to the part they were still proving up and made a place for Jean to keep the milk and food cool. He had decided that he wanted to live close to the orchard so he could keep out the deer and livestock.

begin here

Ed Applegate had come back in and wanted to work for his board. Merl knew he was a hard worker and proposed that he stay through the summer and, if they got any hunting clients, he would hire Ed to do the packing. Jean apparently had printed up and sent Merl copies of a descriptive brochure she had prepared about the facilities and offerings at their new "Flying W" Ranch. In a section describing the accommodations at the ranch, Jean had written "There are clean comfortable beds in the ranch house or individual tents or cabins, located among the trees by the creek." The cabins may have been something they had talked about and were planning for the future but did not yet exist. Merl wrote that "The booklets are sure fine and they ought to get some results and I know you are right about the cabins but I've got to build a skid road to the timber and get some money to buy some lumber to finish them. I looked the Able [Abel] cabins over again today and it will take lumber to floor them and windows and some kind of wall finish and it is a heck of a long way to walk to meals but I will clean them up if I get time and mabe you can fix them some way when you get here." The "Abel cabins" were about a half mile south of the Wallace cabin. It is likely that these actually were some of the original Caswell structures that were on a piece of the land that Bacon had acquired. Therefore, at this point they did not quite belong to the Wallaces; that would come a couple months later. Furthermore, any property that Abel formerly owned now belonged to Elizabeth Bellingham.

In August 1932, Merl remodeled the "bunk house" and put a new roof and floor on the "little cabin over the ditch" to use for a store house. Presumably, the buildings were still located near the mouth of Spring Creek and the "ditch" referred to was actually the creek. Later the buildings were moved to the Wallace homestead site and were the ones that Dan LeVan in July 1936 described as "the two completed cabins 12 x 14 feet in size." One of these (probably the old Caswell storehouse) was 1½ stories tall and had a loft. Both were suitable for living in year 'round.

During spring 1933 Merl believed he had found "the lost quarter-section marker" that identified the north-south division between Bacon and Abel's land and he determined (probably erroneously) that the Abel house was on his land. There were conflicts between Wallace

(Left) Jean Wallace and son Bill (William Borah Wallace) in front of the small cabin the Wallaces used as a residence on their homestead prior to the reconstruction of the Caswell 1898 Cabin. The small cabin had been moved up from the old Caswell ranch site at the mouth of Spring Creek and was winterized for year 'round use. Photograph from the Wallace Special Collection (filed under MS Accession #2011-03), University of Idaho Library. (Below) Cabin after it had been renovated by Rex Lanham and used as a toolshed. Photograph in 1982 courtesy of the Payette National Forest.

and Bellingham as to who had ownership of the cabin and the right away along the trail on the east side of Cabin Creek between the parcel the Wallaces had purchased from Bacon and the parcel Abel had owned (the so-called "disputed corner") (Bill Wallace personal communication August 2005); Merl treated the critical corridor as though

he owned it because among other things, it provided a crucial link to his Bacon property, to Big Creek, and to the outside.

In early February 1933 Merl and a man named Wy began moving the "Bacon house" north to the center of the former Conyers

(Above) A second small cabin that also was winterized. This one had a loft. In particular, it was used by the Wallaces to house paying guests but never was used as a post office, as some have erroneously claimed. Photograph courtesy of the Payette National Forest. (Right) Inset "Flying W" brand formed with horseshoe nails in an end log of the cabin. Photograph by author.

homestead to become the main Wallace cabin. This building originally was the 1898 Caswell ranch house and had been purchased by the Wallaces in 1931 as part of their acquisition of the Bacon homestead. He thought that with any luck, they would have it up again in 10 days but that would prove overly optimistic. During the spring in 1933 Merl finished the foundation for the "new" house, disassembled the building and moved the logs to the new location with Wy's help. However, three years later, when Dan LeVan visited Cabin Creek on July 9, 1936 to officially inspect the Wallace's homestead claim, the cabin was still not finished. At the time, it was reportedly 18 x 24 feet in size but in 1979 was measured by Wylie et al. as 20' 7" by 22' 2" north to south. It was subdivided into three rooms, had all of the logs in place, and was ready for the shake roof. Presumably the cabin was completed and occupied later in the year. In the process of reconstruction, the east and west walls remained in their original orientation but the north and south ends were swapped.

At the time they were married, Merl was making $150 a month and was counting on another $20 per month from rental of a house, and Jean received $300 for her work as an aide during the state legislative session. After Merl quit his job with the Forest Service, what little savings they had were rapidly expended and the Wallaces were dependent solely on the earnings from the ranch and from Jean's 3-month stint with the legislature. Consequently, especially in their early years at Cabin Creek, Jean would leave for Boise in late fall just before the road over Elk Summit was closed by snow, and not return until after the legislative session concluded at the end of March or often not until after the road opened again around June. In addition, Merl took on a number of other jobs to help make ends meet. In particular, he got the contract to deliver the U.S. mail on the Star Route from Big Creek Village to the Clover Postoffice, which now was located on the Wallace Ranch. In 1938 this contract paid $3360 per year. Depending on the time of year, the job entailed packing the mail by horseback, dogsled, or on foot. By the winter of 1932-1933, Merl had acquired a sled and three dogs. In December 1937, he said of his dogs in a letter to Jean "Old Speck is as good as he ever was and Bing is a dandy and Nig is as good as two dogs."

In the spring of 1932, soon after she had gotten to Cabin Creek, Jean "suffered a nameless illness and foul disposition for weeks." At some point she blew up at Merl, hiked out over Elk Summit, which was still under 7 feet of snow, and was met by family members at Warren, who took her back to Boise. It was several months before she discovered she was pregnant and then her doctor advised her to stay safe and quiet in Boise until after the baby was born. When Merl finally learned of her pregnancy in late August, he was elated. Their son, William [Bill] Borah Wallace was born January 9, 1933 in Boise, while Merl was busy taking care of the livestock and making improvements on the ranch. In mid-March, Merl began making plans with the pilot Bob King to bring Jean and the new baby in by plane from Cascade in about a month, along with some garden tools and groceries. However, they apparently did not arrive before the end of June and left before the end of October. It seems quite likely, from a letter Jean wrote to Merl at the end of May, that she was suffering from postpartum depression.

In mid July 1932 Merl finished most of the haying with the help of two hired hands he paid $1.50 each per day for the 12 days. Sidney Downey also had come in to tend the garden in Jean's absence. They got a good crop of grass hay, about 40 tons, and two cuttings of alfalfa of about four loads each. However, the garden he was counting on for produce proved to be a disappointment. The cows had gotten into the sweet corn while he was occupied with haying, the ground squirrels ate most of the cabbage, and a frost at the end of August killed all of the beans, squash, tomatoes, and remaining sweet corn (though the "squaw" corn was spared).

Merl Wallace's dog sled and team used for winter transportation and delivery of mail. The lead dog is not shown. Merl's brother-, sister-, and mother-in-law are on the sled. Photograph from the Wallace Special Collection (filed under MS Accession #2011-03), University of Idaho Library.

Principal hayfield on the Conyers/Wallace homestead, that was watered by an irrigation ditch along the west side of the Cabin Creek valley, as seen from a landing plane. Site of the original (upper) landing field is just beyond the sunlit area in the center of the photograph. The Wallace cabin is visible to the right of the two tall conifers in the mid right portion of the photograph. Photograph by author.

Also in August, he learned that Jake and Eric Janson had sold the Snowshoe Mine (reportedly for $50,000) to a new company that expected to hire 25 men and promised to purchase all the beef and potatoes Merl could supply. However, he did not get many fishing or hunting clients and by the end of August was taking rather drastic measures to make up the expected shortfall; he began whip sawing lumber to make sluice boxes and a rocker. He wrote Jean "I am going to the small bar just below the cave [at the mouth of Cave Creek] where I found some coarse gold. I figure if I can make $10.00 per day it will beat packing hunters. I will try it for three days and clean up and if it is good I will run the boxes until snow flies." Unfortunately the prospect literally didn't pan out and in September Merl took his horses, including his team of draft animals, up to the mine for couple of weeks to work for pay.

Merl Wallace with his arrangement for hauling pipe to the Snowshoe Mine on Crooked Creek. Photograph from the Wallace Special Collection, University of Idaho Library.

Although currently short of cash, he sent Jean a list of supplies in mid-September that he wanted her to get to him by the first of October, before winter set in. The supplies apparently were intended to last him until spring or later. The list is a good indication of what it took, other than beef or wild game and on-site garden produce, to sustain a working man in the backcountry for 7 or 8 months: 800 lbs of flour, 300 lbs of sugar, 100 lbs of lard, 60 lbs of bacon or two dressed hogs, 200 lbs of beans, 90 lbs of mush oats, 50 lbs of rice, 50 lbs of coffee, 10 lbs of baking powder, 5 lbs of cocoa, 2 lbs of pepper, 25 lbs of table salt, 1 bottle of vanilla extract and 1 bottle of lemon extract, 24 cartons of matches, 4 dozen candles, mantles and 3 generators for lanterns, 10 gallons of gasoline, 10 gallons of coal oil, 24 bars of laundry soap, 24 bars of hand soap, 200 lbs of 30d (penny) nails, 100 lbs of 40d, and 25 lbs each of 6, 8, and 10d nails.

In addition, he needed 500 lbs of block and 400 lbs of crystal salt, 1600 lbs of oats, 1000 lbs of wheat, and 500 lbs of barley for the livestock and chickens. He also asked for his brother-in-law and friend Earl Wallin to bring in 2 boxes each of shells for his 30-06 and 25-35 caliber rifles and 2 frying pans to replace ones stolen at Copper Camp the previous winter. He also noted that Jake Janson had given him most of a saw mill that he planned to pack down to Cabin Creek in a few days.

In early February 1933, Merl traveled down to Dave Lewis' Ranch at the mouth of Trail Creek. "Uncle Dave is awful feeble this winter. He can't get out of the house at all and Joe Davis [an old prospector friend] isn't much better. I went down and cut them some wood last week." By May, Merl had eleven new calves. He had installed a hydroelectric plant at the ranch and was pleased that he was able to use the radio to get news from Boise.

The availability of ranch hands at Cabin Creek was quite tenuous and fluid, even though Merl paid them $1 a day, probably including board. Wy, who lived nearby and in February had helped move the big cabin up to Merl's homestead claim, later became ill and unable to work; in mid-March, one of the two remaining hired hands (Thorp) left when the spring work started; and Merl fired the other. Crandall "came over" to help brand and dehorn the cattle. Wy had recovered by March 19 and Thorp was living with him. By the start of May, another man, Al, was working for Merl "again" at the ranch.

During the spring of 1933 Merl planted tomatoes, cabbages, watermelons, and squash — probably in cold frames to protect them from frost. He also planted a number of fruit and shade trees. In addition, Merl got several work projects for which he was paid and they, on top of the work on the ranch in addition to moving the Caswell cabin, kept him hopping. Two of the for-pay projects involved the construction of new landing strips: one on Soldier Bar 9 miles downstream from Cabin Creek and another at Cabin Creek on the "big meadow," that was separate from the original one on the bench. He also sold and took orders for beef from Dan LeVan of the Forest Service and from Jim Hornberger. At one point he was so elated about these prospects for much-needed income that he exclaimed "If everything in view materializes the depressing [sic] is over at the Flying W."

The work at Soldier Bar was for the Forest Service and the ranger from Big Creek Headquarters, Dan LeVan, helped Merl clear rock off the field. The first landing and takeoff from Soldier Bar was made by Bob Johnson in his new Travelair plane and witnessed by Dan LeVan, Bill Parks, John Cook, and Tom Coski. In May, when Merl got to Goat Creek, across from Soldier Bar to deliver supplies, he discovered that the water in Big Creek was so high that he had to put the stuff across on the overhead cable car extending between the two banks, which took extra time.

The work at Cabin Creek was requested by A. A. Bennett, a pilot who apparently was affiliated with the "Big Ramey" mining outfit. He called the first week in May and asked Merl to build a landing field at Cabin Creek. The company planned to fly equipment and supplies to the new field and then pack them to the site. It was a 2-way field, approximately 900 feet long, that took Merl about ten days to construct and left him pleased with the final product. In June, he finished planting the garden, weeded the potatoes, irrigated, and brought in a new batch of laying hens.

In August, Elizabeth Bellingham came in to check on her ranch. Jean and Billy also were at Cabin Creek by then and Elizabeth paid the family a visit. Although her visit apparently was a social one, it had deeper implications that would not become evident for another two years. After Jean returned to Boise, she began the paperwork for obtaining a water right for the Flying W. She found that there were no filings on record for either Cabin Creek or Cow Creek ". . . so Mrs. B has no more water right than a Jackrabbit . . . ." Based on figures Merl sent her at the end of October, Jean estimated (at an apparent rate of 100 inches per 30 acres) 150 inches or 3 cubic feet for the homestead (100 inches in the high ditch across the creek from the homestead cabin, 50 in the ditch taken out at the cabin) and 300 inches (6 cubic feet) for the Bacon place (including 100 inches in the ditch that went behind the Bacon house). But she sent him the form to check her figures and to complete before mailing it in.

In November, Merl faced the harsh realities of a poor market for cattle and no money and contemplated working at the mine on Meadow Creek (Stibnite) for the winter. To add to their problems both Merl at Cabin Creek and Jean and Billy in Boise had to contend with infestations of bed bugs, which they confronted by changing and boiling the bedding, scrubbing with Lysol, and the use of itch medicine. Starting around Thanksgiving, Merl undertook a job for Dan LeVan of the Forest Service to extend the telephone line from the ranch to the Middle Fork of the Salmon River, including a connection at Dave Lewis' Ranch. It took him about 17 days to complete the task, for which he received $68. By the time Merl paid his grocery bill to Homer LeVander in Yellow Pine, he had only $4 or $5 left and still needed $20 to get Bennett to fly in salt. He wrote Jean "I don't see how I can come out Xmas unless I can get some more money . . ." and ended with "If you can help me finance a trip mabe [sic] I can come [for their son's first Christmas and birthday]."

Spring 1934 was a busy time at the ranch, as usual. In early March, Merl hauled hay and skidded in wood with his work team. In the process, he broke all of his single-trees and had to make some more out of "thorn bush" [Hawthorn]. On March 12 he wrote Jean "I am all alone now [i.e., no hired hands] and it is sure fine. I believe I can get more done. This week I will finish the wood and haul the manure. I've got to split 1000 posts yet this spring and plant the garden, clean the ditches, build and repair fences and brand the calves." "Uncle Dave was up last Monday and he is better than he has been for a long time. We argued politics and the cause of the depression and he went home quite happy." Near the end of March Merl wrote that he was occupied with getting the garden in, keeping the mice from eating up the plants in the hotbed, and caring for the cattle and chickens. "I wish you were here to take care of them [hens and chicks]. I've got too many chores." "I gave Wy notice to move out of the Abel house and he is moving up to the Bellingham house. I am going to tear the Abel house down to use it in the new one." In addition, within the next couple of weeks he had 19 new calves to help deliver and look after. During the first two weeks in April, Merl also went down and put in Dave Lewis' crop in exchange for the use of "old Bill."

April apparently marked a sea change in Merl and Jean's relationship when Merl became fed up with having to carry the weight of the ranch operations, especially during the spring-time rush, and then in addition having Jean scold him, as captured in these excerpts from two of his letters:

April 16, 1934 — "Dear Jean & Billy. I got your letter with your demands and I am doing my best but the hay & cattle come first. I do everything

I can between 5 Am. & 9 Pm. but I am telling you once and for all this is going to be the last year I will stay alone and try to raise a garden & chickens. This old world is a big one & I think I can find a place more pleasant." "I don't play the radio much any more because when I do a days work, cook, eat, feed the chickens, milk the cows, and tend to the hotbed I feel like going to bed." And, as he often did, he included a not-so-veiled hint that she should come in soon. "That road will be open in about 30 days if you want to come in that way. Bob King is coming in in a few days after 2 or 3 passengers and I can finance the trip with him if you can come in with him. I would sure love to have Billy with me. Hug and kiss him for me. Love Dad."

May 13, 1934 — Still no Jean. "Well I am still aboard and healthy and have most of the crops in. The early stuff is all up and the next thing will be weeds." "I am planting most of the garden up here so I can watch it." "I want you to come in right away . . . from Yellowpine almost to Profile summit and I will meet you there with the horses as lots of horses are going over now on a well broken trail and if you think it is dangerous for Bill I can walk and carry him as there is only about a mile of snow. Now if you really want to come in early the summit wont be in your way. I haven't got any money, shoes, overalls or shirts but I can go barefoot and make me a buckskin suit." "Chic Walker brought Mr. Fisher and Mr. Fenton in to look at the Ramey placer ground and I asked Mr. Fisher for a job on the Warren dredge and he said he would find something for me if I wanted to go to work. I can't see anything but loneliness, privation, and trouble here & I am ready to quit and pull out at the first opportunity. I won't attempt to fix up your tent as I know it won't be right."

There are no other letters from Merl until November 28 so she presumably got the message.

In his November 28 letter, Merl revealed a couple of additional aspects of his tenuous financial condition. He had gotten a fine work team of black mules named Mike and Molly but then rented them to Jim [Hornberger?]. He told Jean they had earned $60 already. He also told her that he still owed money to Homer LeVander, the store owner in Yellow Pine. Apparently her mother had sent LeVander $50 and Merl promised to get him another $75 by December 15. The mail now was coming from Cascade to Big Creek Village by plane, thus making it possible for Merl to reliably send and receive letters and other items during the winter, as long as he could get them to Headquarters. In a note added on December 9, he told Jean that he would come to Boise in about a week. There is no indication of how long Merl was away or who might have looked after the livestock but among the personal effects of Joe Bayok in the Central Idaho Historical Museum is a photograph with a caption indicating that Joe spent Christmas in one of the Wallaces' two completed cabins in Merl's absence.

There is no record of written correspondence between Jean and Merl during 1935, suggesting the possibility that she took his threat of April 1934 to heart and was at the ranch most of the time, taking up some of the slack. They are likely to have continued to struggle to make ends meet, though Merl would have felt the benefits of her increased companionship and help with the ranch operations, and the garden and chickens in particular probably blossomed under her care.

However, there are two letters that suggest a further increase in the rift in the relationship between Merl and Elizabeth Bellingham. The previous August (1934), Dave Lewis had received a letter from her that he quickly showed to his friend Merl. In the letter, Bellingham said she heard that Merl had kept her horse Betty tied up all of the time without food and had worked her horses without shoes. She also told Dave she was looking for someone else to look after her ranch. On September 2, 1934, Merl replied heatedly about her "slanderous accusations" and, perhaps ill-advisedly wrote ". . . you will no doubt realize that the statement you wrote Uncle Dave is sufficient cause for a libel suit and I am certainly surprised that a woman of your intelligence would pass such a statement around without first making sure of its authenticity." Bellingham didn't reply for almost an entire year and when she did, she revealed the depth of the split between them and a threat she is holding over his head. She wrote "I would think you would feel that you owed me a life time of gratitude for considering your financial condition when your dear little wife was expecting a visit from the stork."

"I knew at that time she ought to have more or less things she did not need at any other time in life and I wanted her to have them

so I never asked you for the rest of the money due on the contract &
which is still owed. I know as bright, intelligent and honest a little
wife as she is, your dealings with other people will never meet with
her approval. And in regard to having another talk with me we had
that the year before and I promised you not to say any thing before
Mrs Wallace. and I asked why don't she know any thing about your
business and you said she is so nervous and I gave you my word not
to say any thing about it. but at the breakfast table that morning I
felt guilty not to tell her every thing but I had given you my word
and I proved to you I was a woman of my word. but since I received
your letter I don't think I am under any obligation to keep it any
longer, so she is going to know just how we stand financially some of
these days. Yours truly, Elizabeth Bellingham."

Also, on March 19, 1934, after determining to his satisfaction
that the Abel house was on his property, Merl had torn it down in
order to use the material on their own house. On September 12, 1935,
probably in response to this action and Bellingham's recent threat,
Merl received a typed notice from Henry Schied, stating that by
direction of Jess Warner [who was now living on the Bellingham
place], he had moved eleven 12-foot and four short logs, the property
of Mrs. Elizabeth Bellingham, from the premises of Merl Wallace
to the property of Mrs. Bellingham. These logs later may have been
used in the construction of the two-story cabin that was built on
the Bellingham place for Jess and Vernie Warner and their children.

Merl's friend "uncle" Dave Lewis was getting up in age and in-
creasingly subject to ill health. He regularly had offers to buy his
place, including one in about 1927 from Harry Shellworth for $6000,
whenever Dave was through with it. It is not known whether Harry
was acting in his own behalf or in his official capacity as land agent
for the Boise Payette Lumber Company. But in July 1935 Dave accepted an offer from Jess Taylor for $1200 plus the right to continue
to live on the place as long as he wanted. However, near the end
of 1935, Taylor became concerned about Dave's deteriorating condition and sought to formalize their agreement. Someone was needed
to witness the signing of the contract and normally Merl Wallace
would have been the logical one to ask, since he and Dave were

good friends and he was Dave's closest neighbor. Apparently Merl was unavailable so they asked Walt Estep, who was in the area and had been until recently their next closest neighbor at Acorn Creek. After the signing, they gave Estep the document to take to Cascade for filing.

On the trail midway between the Lewis and Wallace ranches was a small flat where Frank Lobear (a.k.a. Lobauer) was living. Lobear had once worked for Estep on a mining claim on Ramey Ridge but the two had a falling out, reportedly due in part to the fact that Estep once had an prolonged affair with Lobear's wife. Unfortunately for Estep, Lobear was waiting for him and, after an argument, shot him in the neck as he turned to leave Lobear's wall tent, killing him instantly. Afterward, Lobear went to the Lewis Ranch and confessed that he had "shot Estep." Apparently Jess Taylor wasn't home, so Estep spoke to his wife Ann, who notified the authorities.

The telephone call from the Lewis ranch went to Headquarters, where Noel Routson was on duty, and the message was then conveyed to the sheriff in Cascade. However, at that point it only was known that Estep had been "shot" and not that he was dead. The sheriff wanted to get someone to the scene as quickly as possible to determine Estep's condition and render assistance. The closest source of help still was Cabin Creek, even though Merl was away. Routson must have known that Myron McCoy was there, taking care of the Flying W ranch and packing the mail, and he was contacted by telephone. Myron got Jess Warner from the Bellingham ranch to go with him. When they arrived at the scene of the murder, Myron recalled in a 1984 interview, "They could see right away quick that Estep was dead. He had been shot in the back of the neck and the bullet had come out of his mouth. There was a lot of blood all over the snow." Myron stayed there all night waiting for the sheriff and coroner to arrive. Among Estep's belongings, they found Dave Lewis' deed of sale and it was eventually recorded. Myron was given the task of packing Estep's body out to Big Creek over the next couple of days.

It appears (based on a January 11, 1936 letter from Merl to Jean) that Merl had joined his family in Boise for Christmas and left Myron McCoy in charge of the ranch. Then Merl came back alone to deliver the mail and help Myron but first stopped off at the county jail in Cascade to visit Lobear. Frank admitted to Merl that he might have shot Estep in the back. Later, Merl wrote Jean of his meeting "He said he [Lobear] turned just as he shot him." Lobear was convicted of manslaughter and sent to the state penitentiary in Boise in June 1936. But five years later he was pardoned and in 1949 made his way back to Big Creek. At some point, perhaps early the next summer, Lobear on his way to his mining claim north of Ramey Ridge was given a ride down to Beaver Creek by Forest Service employee Bob McCoy, where the road was closed by snow. He was never seen alive again. On July 15, 1950 Billy Wallace wrote Jean from Little Ramey Creek that "Old Frank Lobar is lost on Ramey Ridge a variety of folks searched for him to no avail."

Merl had expected Jean and Billy to return by plane in early to mid-February in 1936, but they still hadn't arrived by the 25th. By then Myron had left to resume work with a Forest Service trail crew and Merl had to get the Warner girls to do the chores while he was away. In addition, Merl's expectation of seeing Jean and Billy in February suggests that she was not working during the legislative session.

About the time Dave Lewis died in June 1936, Jess Taylor's wife ran off with his partner Cal Williams. Jess caught up with them at Cabin Creek and gave Cal a beating, for which Jess was later incarcerated for a while in Cascade. After Ann left, Jess returned to Boise and worked as a building contractor for the next 12 years during which time the Lewis/Taylor ranch probably was occupied only sporadically by various caretakers or leasers.

When the Big Creek district ranger Dan Levan stopped by on July 9 to do the final inspection on the Wallaces' homestead claim, he reported that the "Family is living on claim, haying, gardening, two cabins completed, one under construction, household furniture, plows, harrow, mowing machine, ditcher, hay rake, wagon, work team, harness, milk cows, and chickens." LeVan also recorded the presence of 16 cattle, 8 horses, 4 hogs, and 80 chickens. "There are 18 acres [of irrigated ground] producing crops, 1 acre of garden, [and] 60 mixed fruit trees 3 years old." There was another 10 acres of agricultural land and the rest was grazing land. In addition, the Wallaces had a permit to graze the cattle and horses at large on Forest Service land. LeVan estimated that the hay crop would amount to about 10 tons of alfalfa and 5 tons of oats. He also estimated that there was 1½ miles of 3-strand barbed wire fence. Based on his observations, LeVan recommended that the Wallaces be awarded the patent to their claim.

Merl continued to deliver the mail in 1937, in addition to running the stock ranch and guiding an occasional client. The Wallaces successfully completed their "proving up" period during the year and received the patent on the original Conyers homestead portion of their property. By mid-December, Jean and Billy had returned to Boise. Jean found the winter to be "pretty dreary" and remarked in a letter to George Nay a potential client about her experience that "The few people who live in the [Big Creek] country in the winter are trappers or miners, there is very little communication, skiing or snowshoeing or trips with dog teams are undertaken not as a sport but as bitter necessity, and there is a general tendency to huddle around the red hot stoves and only venture out to get more wood. Our winter ranch work is feeding cattle, not especially thrilling." When Merl wrote Jean and Billy on the 13th, it had been raining for 3 days and Cabin and Big Creeks were in full flood. Merl was afraid to take the mules to deliver mail and instead was going to pack the mail on his back this week. During the next ten days he also worked on building a hog house and a small barn for the team and cows. He thought some of the pigs would be ready to butcher by about January 1st. The chickens were producing a total of only 2 eggs a day. In addition, there were some turkeys and guinea fowl. "One of the 'guinnies' is dead — I think the gobbler killed him. They were fighting a lot." He had one more mail trip to make with the mules and then planned to go back to using the dogs.

1938 was much the same as the preceding three years regarding the limited correspondence between Merl and Jean and suggesting that she and Billy may have been at the ranch for most of the year. In particular there was no forewarning of the financial crisis and apparent life-changing event they would confront in August. In fact, the beginning of the year suggested just the opposite, although in a March 20 letter, Merl indicated that he was not carrying the mail anymore and that Joe Powell was using the dogs to deliver it instead. He wrote "I run short of hay and I had to stay at home and herd the cattle and look after all the stock." But by the end of March 1938 Jean and Merl had begun using some new stationery they had made for the ranch that seems to describe well their situation and plans. In the center of the letterhead under the main banner "FLYING W RANCH" is the subheading "Most Remote Ranch in America." Above them on the left are the captions in smaller fonts: "BIG GAME HUNTING; Elk, Deer, Goats, and Sheep; Shots Guaranteed" and matching them on the right are: "FINE FISHING; Summer Pack Trips; Ranch Guests; Private Landing Field." Their assertion of the exceptional isolation of their ranch, seems to have gone unchallenged and could well have been correct. As support for their claim the Wallaces, in their promotional brochure, cited a United States Geodetic Survey party, operating near the junction of the Middle Fork and main Salmon River a few years earlier, as calling this "the most remote section in the United States," on account of its inaccessibility, the few roads entering it, and the actual distance from railroads, telephone, and telegraph.

Jean and Billy arrived at the ranch some time after the first week of April in 1938. In the meantime, Merl stopped working the mail route around the end of February and focused on the cattle. They were not doing well and the hay was going fast. Merl was busy cutting a few logs to build a dining room onto the kitchen. But actual construction was on hold until he could get the crops planted and the upper meadow fenced. March was the usual frenzy of activity. Merl was ordering the garden seeds and the cattle, horses, and pigs were all about to give birth.

Near the end of March, Merl learned that he had gotten the bid for the Yellow Pine-Big Creek mail route for $3360 but had been unsuccessful on the more lucrative Cascade — Stibnite Route. In his letter to Jean on March 30, he wrote "I am glad you are coming into the ranch by plane as it will be impossible to go to Hdqrs. with mules for a month yet. The snow is all gone here and the landing field is dry. The buttercups have been blooming for a week but it has been blustery and the grass is slow getting started but the cattle are doing fine and good prospects for a good calf crop. I think Lady is going to have a colt this spring. If no bad luck overtakes us we will have 4 colts." "The pigs are sure fat & sassy. The biggest one is snow white and I have already made a pet out of him." "You mentioned the supplies. We have a lot of the staples as flour, sugar, etc. but we will need some soda, baking powder, coffee, lemon extract, and nutmeg. I will try to get some money up at Hdqrs for some barley and fence staples."

Among the few items in the Wallace file for 1938 is a mortgage between Merl & Jean and Gaylord Baldwin dated August 16. They had put essentially all of their tangible assets on the line in order to borrow a $1000 under the usurious terms of 8% interest due in only three months! They must have been desperate for the money because there is nothing to indicate they had ever gotten beyond the subsistence level in the seven years they had been operating the ranch. Even Jean's former job with the legislature at $100 per month (during a period outside of the terms of the mortgage) and Merl's former salary with the Forest Service at $150 would not have garnered them the amount needed in three months, even if they had no other expenses! What could have triggered such drastic action and without apparent warning? The most plausible explanation, is that Elizabeth Bellingham had called in the note she had been holding.

They mortgaged the 300 acres of land, all the buildings, and all 10 of their Decker pack saddles and rigging. Also included were all of the livestock consisting of: their seven most dependable horses 6-12 years old (including Blaze, Dolly, Dude, Mollie, Patches, & Sleepy), three colts and one 3 year old black mare of their own breeding, ten miscellaneous mules, mares, and geldings 5-10 years old branded "OX", 16 Durham and Herford cows, 2-4 years old, and 10 Durham and Hereford calves, 1-6 months old. Gaylord must already have been counting his good fortune and smiling all the way to the bank! Given their past performance, Merl and Jean seem doomed to failure and the loss of almost everything they owned and had worked so hard for.

But some how they managed to hang on for another 9 months and in May 1939 Jean's mother Annabelle Orr came to their rescue and assumed the loan. However, though the fate of the ranch was secured, they never seemed to regain their equilibrium and seemed to lose all hope of ever turning a profit on the actual operations of the ranch. There is no known record of activities on the Wallace ranch in 1939 but one can speculate that the problems that brought on their financial crisis the previous August had not been resolved. Jean indicated in her autobiography that after she and Billy came out for the winter they intended to stay out only a couple of months, but Billy started kindergarten and did so well, and a State House job opened up for Jean and they needed money, so she stayed out during 1940. Merl also had to seek off-site employment for them to survive.

These actions effectively marked the end of their lives at Cabin Creek as a family. A May 6, 1940 letter from Merl to Jean (the only one for the year) indicates that he had been working at the Snowshoe Mine on Crooked Creek but that day it ". . . has shut down indefinitely and the last of the crew went out today. We are hoping they pay up." It is not known what all he did while the mine was closed. He continued with the mail route, probably returned to Cabin Creek, and may have taken on packing and other jobs with the Forest Service. However, when Merl wrote Jean on February 3, 1941, the mill at the mine had resumed operating the previous day and presumably he was rehired and worked there until just after the start of World War II.

It appears that Merl left for Seattle before Christmas 1941 and hired on with a contractor to the US Navy (Siems Drake Puget Sound). The company was responsible for building Naval airbases in Alaska and Merl was employed to drive truck at $1.40 an hour. Merl finally was receiving a regular paycheck, possibly the first since he had left the Forest Service, and was sending part of it to Jean and Billy. Merl leased the ranch to George McCoy and the cattle were sold to George "Blondie" McGill. McCoy stayed on the ranch until the spring of 1943. He and McGill purchased the former Stonebraker, Beale, and Hotzel ranches in

Chamberlain Basin and formed a partnership for cattle ranching. In the autumn, they operated hunting camps. The mail route on Big Creek went to Lafe Cox, who shared delivery responsibilities with his wife Emma and his caretaker Jim Carpenter (1883-1964) at Mile High Ranch. By September Merl was at the Naval Air Station in Kodiak, Alaska. He hadn't left too soon because in October War Production Board Order L-208 forced closure of the Snowshoe Mine on Crooked Creek.

Several things could have motivated Merl to join up with the Sea Bees: the need for money and a steady job, patriotism, and discouragement that all the hard work at the ranch had gotten him nowhere. Jean, on the other hand had been insulated from much of the hardship by her ability to retreat to Boise and gain comfort and support from her mother. In the end, Merl essentially had starved out, burned out, and given up.

Jean found a teaching job in Fairfield, Idaho and moved there from Boise with Billy. Her mother withered and died under the strain of the war and her boarding house Gray Gables was sold.

In March 1943, Merl resigned his job in Kodiak with Siems Drake Puget Sound and transferred to a US Corps of Engineers project in Anchorage. In May 1943, Jean received a letter from Joe Powell at Big Creek, describing the dire condition of the stock and ranch at Cabin Creek and offering to take them over for 2 years for half the increase in stock plus some other entice-ments (new mower, etc.). However, about 5 weeks later he wrote again to back out of the deal for a bunch of reasons: he hadn't gotten the mower he requested, the horses had eaten most of the hay crop, he didn't see how he " . . . could make grocery money this year, " he was having bladder problems and might have to see a doctor, and he was already committed to "a half interest in the Taylor Ranch." However, he did offer to look after the place for a small "wadge." Jean wisely decided to visit the ranch and see conditions for herself. She had several offers to rent or buy the place and she wanted to retrieve personal items and some of the horses. After looking things over, she did not concur with Powell's assessment and returned with renewed resolve to hang on to the ranch as long as she could.

Soon after Jean returned from Cabin Creek, she wrote Merl a poignant letter dated September 1, 1943.

> "*Dearest Merl:*
>
> *I just got back from the ranch. We had such a wonderful time, riding our horses & fishing. We stayed at Jake's* [Janson] *a few days until we could get down, then we were alone for a week, then Lafe Cox came down and helped us pack up & brought us out. He is to bring out the stuff I took away next week. I have made an arrangement with him to cut the hay & and watch the house and if I do not sell the place he will fix the fences & put up the hay & take care of the place next year too. I had about arranged to sell to Art & Margaret* [Frances, who in 1940 were living at the Snowshoe Mine] *for $3500 before I went down, but after I got there, Merl, I just couldn't go thru with it. The house & all the things & the horses are there just like we left them & it seemed to me it wasn't right to sell & turn loose of a place that was what we wanted so much. We can never get another one like it.*
>
> *The horses were in pretty good shape. George* [McCoy] *did not do as much stealing as Joe said, apparently, and it was your stuff that suffered. (I couldn't find much in the way of accounts, papers etc, at the ranch, they had put them in the attic & the rats had done their worst.) There are 5 mules including Andy, Jenny & Donny. Joe* [Powell?] *is wintering Andy & Jenny. The pinto stallion is there and the appalossie & Sleepy are OK, in good shape. Maggie is there with a fine colt, but is fistulated* [abscessed]. *Jim Carpenter & Lafe are taking her up to Mile High to doctor.*
>
> *I have the black mare Thelma, and John, and a 3 or 4 year old filly. Thelma has a year old black colt that is a beauty, Lafe will brand him for me. The filly has a nice colt. There is a 3 yr. old gelding there that is the picture of the old black mare & I think is her colt but he is branded with George's brand & was sold & got away & came back. The fellows said George was supposed to have won that colt in a poker game. They also told me George sold the good milk cow this spring & said he won her from you in a crap game. Well _____ what can I do about that?*
>
> *I have all sorts of offers on the place, to rent etc. I would like to keep it, as I said, it just doesn't seem like we should let it go. We could use what we make in these times to fix it up. But if you don't think you would want to*

go back on it of course it would be better to sell it. . . .

I wish you would send me some money, & tell me if you <u>really</u> want to give up the ranch or hold on to it. When I was there I was just <u>sick</u> about selling it & Billy wants to keep it & the horses. He rode Patches & was just wild about it all.

I suppose I am a fool to hold on to an old dream. But the place must have something, or so many others wouldn't want it. Bob Johnson wants it, too.

Write me, & send that wages estimate right away.

Love

Jean

Lafe is taking care of the saddles, too & the deckers & will watch the place. Joe is sort off in his head & wants me to sell to Bob Johnson, so he can work for Bob."

Although the letter was initially returned for lack of a correct box number, Merl received the news of Jean's decision on October 7 and wrote "I got your most welcome letter . . . and I was sure tickled about you not selling the ranch. After I signed the power of attorney I was sorry and I felt the same way about the place as you said you did. After all I put in a lot of hard labor and we've had some grief and still it is home."

Instead of selling the ranch, Jean leased it to Lafe Cox, who put Jim Carpenter there to look after it. But Jean and Merl's mutual attachment to Cabin Creek would prove insufficient to hold them togehter for much longer. In her autobiography Jean wrote "In 1944 the Army released the restrictions which had prevented the families of civilian workers from going to Alaska, and Merl wanted us to be there. He was sold on Alaska. So we got ready to go on the first boat we could get . . . ." "We sailed for Alaska on August 29, 1944 and on August 30, 1945 Billy and I sailed back again, after a year of adventures in the Frozen North, some of which were pleasant but some others of which would make your hair stand on end. And I was a free woman, my husband having succumbed to the wiles of an Aleut squaw . . . ." Two weeks before she left, Merl gave her his interest in the property. They separated in 1945 and divorced in 1946.

In 1947, Jean leased the Flying W Ranch to Lester Curtis an outfitter, with the agreement to raise horses on shares and to allow Billy to spend the summers there learning about horses and forests and that Jean could spend vacations there with saddle and pack horse available for any trips she wanted to make. Billy [ages 13-20 during the time Curtis was there] also helped with the haying and other ranch operations. Eventually Jean and Bill brought out some of the saddle horses, notably the Appaloosa Patches; joined a riding club; and gave lessons to children. Curtis continued to oversee the Flying W Ranch into 1953, while also operating a hunting guide service, packing for U.S. Forest Service, mining, and contracting the mail service on the Star route from the Big Creek Store. In December 1951, when mail service from Big Creek ended, he was the last horseback mail carrier to Cabin Creek. During the early 1950s, he and Bill Sullivan had a hunting camp contract with Jess Taylor and wintered their horses on hay at the Taylor Ranch (formerly the Dave Lewis place). Jean recalled in her autobiography that for her and Bill "These were golden years, but they ended when Billy, who had decided to make Forestry his career, went to the University and married Mickie Billman, one of the girls who used to ride with us."

Les decided he no longer wanted to operate the ranch, if Billy wasn't going to be there to help, so "in a moment of insanity" Jean agreed to sell it and her share of the horses to Rex E. Lanham, a developer who earlier had purchased the Middle Fork Lodge and later sold it to the Las Vegas gambling magnate Bill Harrah. The initial purchase by Lanham, completed on July 25, 1953, was under the cover of Powerline Construction Company of Pocatello, Idaho, in which he was a co-partner with Pete Sorenson. In November 1959 Jean received the final payment from Lanham on the ranch escrow. Lanham chose to continue to use the "Flying W Ranch" name.

Les Curtis and Jean Orr Wallace were married in 1957 and she moved back to Big Creek country where he still had a mine and a guide and packing business. They also bought a ranch up the Boise River to serve as winter quarters and soon were in the cattle business. Jean felt that all she had left of the Big Creek backcountry was the [unpatented] Sunlight Mine at Little Ramey, which eventually would be included within an impending wilderness boundary.

Les Curtis, caretaker of the Wallace ranch in the early 1950s and eventual second husband of Jean Wallace. Photograph provided by Richard H. Holm Jr.

History of the Caswell Ranch House at Cabin Creek

The Caswell ranchhouse built in 1898 at the mouth of Spring Creek as it appeared in July 1901. Note that the doorway on the end facing the viewer (south) is off center to the west and that the only side door is facing east. Photograph by Luman Caswell from an album owned by his grandson Stewart Taylor.

The Caswell ranchhouse in about 1903. Photograph by Luman Caswell from an album owned by his grandson Stewart Taylor.

The Caswell ranchhouse in about 1910 after the ranch was purchased by John Conyers. Conyers, Dave Lewis, and Charlie Myers are in the photograph. Photograph (MG190 #50) from Dave Lewis Special Collection (MS Accession #2011-03), University of Idaho Library.

Similar view as 1901 photograph as seen in June 2013, eighty years after the building had been moved. Photograph by Charles R. Peterson.

The former Caswell 1898 cabin (the annex portion of the ranchhouse added several years later is no longer present) in the 1930s after being disassembled in spring 1933 and moved further up Cabin Creek to the site of the Merl & Jean Wallace homestead. The presence of a roof indicates that the photograph was taken after July 1936. Note that the doorway on the near (south) end is now located in the center of the wall and that the side door retains its original position, indicating that north and south walls have been switched from their original locations. Photograph courtesy of the Payette National Forest.

After Lanham purchased the Wallace ranch, he constructed a massive stone fireplace on the south end that covered the former doorway, extended the window on the right to the southeast corner, and added a laundry room along the west wall. Photograph taken in 1974, courtesy of the Payette National Forest.

The cabin as it appeared in 2009. After the Forest Service purchased it, they restored the original window opening in the southeast end, replaced the Lanham-era single-thickness metal roof with a wooden shingle one, and removed the laundry room addition. The lilac bush by the south east corner, planted in the 1930s, still survives. Photograph by author.

A flurry of building activity occurred on Cabin Creek starting soon after the establishment of two well-financed guest ranches. Shown here are the early construction stages of Hollenbeak's lodge (above) and barn (below) in the late 1950s. Photographs from the collection of Kathy (Hollenbeak) Kough provided by Richard H. Holm Jr.

The Dude Ranchers

U p until about the 1950's livestock, both horses and cattle, provided a major source of livelihood to occupants on Cabin Creek and required year 'round residence; feed and construction materials were largely obtained on site; and a substantial amount of food was home grown. In addition, paid "guests" — whether fishers, hunters, horseback riders, or simply vacationers — played a secondary role in the operations and income. Frugality and self sufficiency prevailed.

But all of that changed with the dramatic shift in socioeconomic conditions following World War II. The national economy boomed, livestock raising shifted to large feedlots and big ranches, where the economies of scale prevailed. People left the rural areas and flocked to the cities and suburbs where there were fewer physical hardships and modern amenities were readily available. Heavy demand for new homes helped fuel the economy and drove up the need for lumber. In particular, the logging industry shifted from selective logging and sustainable yields to clear cuts and other industrial-style operations and began to show huge profits.

People in general had more expendable income and more time for relaxation. However, they also grew more selective and impatient about the use of that time and no longer were willing to invest a large proportion of it just to reach a recreational destination or one that might not include the whole family. In such settings the airplane provided a critical link. Places like Cabin Creek, with an existing airstrip, were ideally positioned to be developed for this type of recreation. To those with significant outside income and access to airplanes, the place was much less isolated. Owners, their families, hired hands, and guests all could access the area in less than an hour from places like Cascade, Salmon, or Challis, which in turn also could be reached easily by airplane or on paved roads by automobile.

Large amounts of modern construction materials such as milled lumber, particle board, prefabricated doors and large windows, metal roofing, and hundreds of sacks of premixed concrete could be gotten in easily. Also, with availability of relatively frequent and dependable flights, fresh fruits and vegetables and other groceries were relatively easy to obtain. Bulk supplies of staple food items sufficient to last months and large gardens were no longer essential. Whole families or parties of people could enjoy the bonus of an flight over spectacular scenery and effortless delivery to the point where their sought-after relaxation or recreational activity began. Even the mail arrived weekly by air beginning in 1952 and, along with it on a space-available basis, supplies and relatively inexpensive passenger service.

These trends worked against the former way of life at Cabin Creek and produced a relatively rapid change from self-supporting ranches and year 'round residence to recreational use and part-time residence by the owner, generally with a hired hand or so to look after the ranch from late fall to early summer. An added incentive to the development of amenities attractive to the more adventurous vacationers was the discovery by astute investors that land, scenic settings, and access to an abundance of fish and game could be purchased relatively cheaply from starved out in-holders within choice locations such as the Idaho Primitive Area. For a few select individuals this offered the opportunity for profitable investment and a chance to write off taxes on other parts of their businesses as development costs on this new venture.

Although the Wallaces (and possibly the Mabees and their successor Gordon Ray on the former Bellingham Ranch) had intended to develop the recreational aspects of their sequestered location as a major part of their ranching operations, those dreams never fully materialized. They simply lacked the financial resources to bring to reality their dream of ranching and catering to paid clients on the last frontier and actually turning a profit.

The same year that Jean Wallace leased the Flying W Ranch to Les Curtis, Elizabeth Bellingham passed away. The year that Jean sold out to Rex Lanham was only three years before Gordon Ray sold the Abel/Bellingham property to Loren K. Hollenbeak for $30,000 in 1956. It seems that Hollenbeak and Ray had first met

Lanham's motel (above) and barn (below) in 1977. Photographs courtesy of the Payette National Forest.

through business dealings related to logging; Hollenbeak also may have been a hunting client of Ray's.

It is difficult to separate the specific changes made by Lanham and Hollenbeak during the period of joint occupancy but some insight can be obtained from a list of structures associated with their centers of operations at the time of a 1982 inventory by the US Forest Service. When Lanham purchased the Flying W, he acquired the Wallaces main cabin (formerly the Caswell ranch house), a small bunkhouse, a "tool shed" (formerly used by the Wallaces as a residence and later for guests), and a root cellar. There also likely was a power house, hydroelectric generator, and dam; a spring house; and an outhouse. The existing main cabin was remodeled by Lanham in 1955 and a large cobblestone fireplace was added to the south end, which covered one of the three entrances, and an interior ceiling of tongue-and-groove knotty pine boards was installed.

A concrete floor and metal roof also are attributed to him. Lanham eventually also added a board & batten laundry annex to the west side of the Wallace cabin. He had four new log structures constructed: a lodge, a "Manager's" cabin, a 4-unit "Motel," and a cabin for him and his family. In addition, he had built a combination garage & shop and a pole barn with areas for hay storage, four stalls, and a tack room with racks for 16 saddles. The Lanhams lived in the Caswell/Wallace cabin

Hollenbeak's lodge under construction in 1958. The near part of the building is the original two-story Warner/Bellingham cabin. Photograph from the collection of Kathy (Hollenbeak) Kough provided by Richard H. Holm Jr.

Hollenbeak barn in the late 1950s still undergoing construction. It eventually was painted red and given a shiny metal roof. Photograph courtesy of the Payette National Forest.

until 1961, then moved into their new cabin. The lodge was framed-in and in usable form by 1960. The new log buildings were built from trees cut along Big Creek between the Vines/Ritchey place and Cabin Creek, beginning in 1957. The logs were floated down to Cabin Creek and then pulled up to the building site with horses. Some of the rough-sawn lumber from Hollenbeak's sawmill was used for the roof of the lodge but most of the other lumber used on the Lanham place was flown in because, as his daughter Cathy Gillihan said, they "didn't want him to cut any more yellow pine."

When Hollenbeak purchased the former Bellingham/Abel Ranch, there were at least three existing buildings — the original "prove up" cabin, where Abel was residing when he was killed; the two-story log cabin built around 1935 for the Warners; and an old stable. Hollenbeak created a sort of "hotel" for his guests by utilizing the existing two-story cabin and expanding it with an addition that was more than twice the size of the original cabin. He also added two one-bedroom frame residences for his hired help that reportedly were built by a crew of visiting loggers in a day or two. In addition, he built a hangar and a large barn with stalls, tack room, and hay storage area. Much of the lumber used in construction of the buildings was manufactured on site with his sawmill. According to Hollenbeak's daughter Kathy Kough [during a telephone conversation with Richard Holm in January 2012], the place barely had running water when they moved in, what they had was piped directly from the creek to the main house. But later Hollenbeak

Hollenbeak sawmill. Photograph courtesy of the Payette National Forest.

"dammed up the creek on the upper end to control flow and built a reservoir" to provide water for the buildings and for irrigation. This same system may have supplied water to the field on the bench where the original runway was located.

Loren, his wife Diana, and their four daughters first resided at their new Cabin Creek ranch after the school session ended in the spring of 1957. However, like the Lanhams, they never lived there year 'round. He and Diana did not like pintos so they replaced them with solid-colored horses and renamed the place simply "Cabin Creek Ranch." They also didn't need as many horses as had been there previously and sold off seven head at the time of purchase.

The Lanham and Hollenbeak acquisitions represented a major shift in operational goals, from livestock to dude ranching, and in levels

(Left) Harvesting and (below) baling hay on the Cabin Creek ranches. Photographs from the collection of Kathy (Hollenbeak) Kough provided by Richard H. Holm Jr.

of financing. Lanham was co-owner of the Powerline Company, and in fact the original purchase of the Flying W was made through it. Hollenbeak owned a logging company under his name based in Hayfork, California and, like Lanham, had a lot more financial latitude than previous owners. Therefore, both Hollenbeak and Lanham had the capabilities for positioning their expenses and losses within a larger corporate setting than just their personal finances. Unlike the Wallaces, Lanham (and Powerline) and Hollenbeak (and his logging company) had the means to put into practice their dreams for developing the ranch. Between them much of the irrigation system and most or all of the hay fields were restored and new barns and corrals built. But mainly their two places were run during the summer and fall as guest ranches. They improved the hunting and fishing guide services, added substantially to the facilities for guests, and improved the airfield. Eventually the place began to resemble a small village.

Ford 8N tractor and McCormick side-delivery rake used for haying at Cabin Creek during the 1950s and 60s. Photograph courtesy of the Payette National Forest.

By the mid 1950s, Lanham and Hollenbeak were running the commercial side of their Cabin Creek holdings primarily as outfitting facilities rather than as livestock ranches. However, their visions for the actual operations of the two places differed substantially. According to his daughter Kathy (Hollenbeak) Kough (in a telephone conversation with Richard Holm in January 2012), "Hollenbeak liked the ranch as a place to get away from things. He liked to rough it at the ranch. He felt that Lanham brought a lot of 'flat landers' to the area and created 'a dude ranch atmosphere.' Hollenbeak felt that these guests did not appreciate the primitive aspect of the place and did not really belong."

Although the Wallaces, Mabees, and Gordon Ray had made use of airplanes in their operations, they were limited by their lack of wealth and inability to own and fly their own plane. Both Hollenbeak and Lanham were pilots and owned small planes and made full use of them for passengers, including clients, and freight at Cabin Creek. Hollenbeak had a Cessna 180 and was more conservative in its use than was Lanham. Lanham actually owned or had access to several kinds of planes suitable for small airfields, some as large as the 9-passenger De Havilland Twin Otter owned by his friend Harrah. Much of Lanham's flying was done before the Cessna 206 became available. However, he preferred the 206 because its large cargo doors enabled it to carry large and bulky items. Often the freight (such as lumber, windows, and doors) was tied on the outside of the planes. He had a Piper Cub with a rack made underneath to carry some items. Johnson Flying Service out of McCall, Idaho had a Travel Air and transported a lot of the big items in the early days. The Travel Air probably hauled Lanham's two jeeps, some of the tractors, and a backhoe. The jeeps were stripped down and cut in half for the flight, then welded back together and reassembled at the ranch. Some of the bulkier items were taken by road to the mouth of Crooked Creek and pulled and slid down Big Creek on the ice in winter.

Overview of Cabin Creek, from the upper end of the inhabited part of the valley in 1972. View is to the south, near the peak of its development. Most of the buildings built by Hollenbeak are evident on the lower right and a few of those built by Lanham (motel & barn) are seen sequestered among the trees just beyond the south end of the runway. Photograph courtesy of Carl Fonnesbeck (shown in scene).

After ten years of operating under the shelter of the Powerline Company, in 1963 Lanham purchased the Wallace (formerly Bacon/ Conyers) property from Powerline. That same year he also obtained the rest of the Cabin Creek property (formerly Abel/Bellingham) from Hollenbeak, allegedly through a Section 1031 tax-free exchange with Hollenbeak. His move may have been motivated by the realization that the area was being considered for national wilderness status that might be expected to enhance the value of the property. Hollenbeak, on the other hand, believed that "the government" was going to force them out and naturalize the place, presumably without adequate compensation.

The series of real estate transactions begun in 1953 ultimately resulted in consolidation of all four of the original homesteads in the hands of Rex Lanham and returned the ranch to a semblance of its size under the Caswells. Lanham operated his Flying W Ranch for a total of 20 years [1953-1974], about the same length of time that Bellingham and the Wallaces each had a presence in the valley. Lanham lived there part-time with his wife Hazel and two daughters Lynda and Catherine, but their principal residence in Emmett, Idaho and sources of income (as also the case with the Hollenbeaks) were largely outside the back country.

Where previous owners had employed a relatively light touch on the land, Hollenbeak and Lanham applied heavy ones. This was not just in the number and size of buildings they constructed, the roads they built, or the motorized vehicles and other equipment they operated; it also was in their attitude toward the land both public and private . For example, Hollenbeak was caught removing timber from National Forest land on Cave Creek over the winter of 1958/1959 for personal use at Cabin Creek, while in later years Lanham was accused of overgrazing public land, including state-owned property at Mile High where, for example, he was alleged to have kept about 40 horses all spring and summer during 1965. Together, they brought in earthmoving equipment, including a bulldozer, and made big changes to the land. Lanham blasted out the rocks from the existing Wallace runway and leveled the Wallace strip with a pull-type road grader when Gordon Ray owned the Bellingham/Abel ranch.

After Hollenbeak bought the place from Ray, he and Lanham brought a 1936 vintage D-8 Caterpillar tractor into Cabin Creek in the summer of 1957. Hollenbeak wanted to use the cat to repair washouts on the road between the airstrip and his fields along Big Creek and to haul logs out of the forest for his sawmill. Lanham needed the cat to repair extensive damage to his hayfield on Cabin Creek Flat caused (probably in the spring of 1956) when Big Creek flooded and cut a new channel, threatening to washout a large portion of the meadow and turn it into cobblestones. To get the Caterpillar to Cabin Creek, they hauled it on a flatbed trailer from Hollenbeak's logging operation near Redding, California to the village of Big Creek then drove it to the end of the road at Crescent Meadow, about three miles beyond the Snowshoe Mine on Crooked Creek. From the meadow, they reportedly had Forest Service approval to walk the cat into the Idaho Primitive Area on roadless federal land. Their route took them up the East Fork of Crooked Creek to the trail up and over Blackburn Saddle and then down Cave Creek to Homsley's old place. Finally, they cut across over Vinegar Hill to

Bulldozer and grader used to maintain the lower runway on Cabin Creek. The dozer, equipped with a blade, also was used to construct a berm and redirect the stream flow along Big Creek, to cut roadways on hillsides along the north side of Cabin Creek Flat east and west of Cabin Creek, and to extend the lower runway. Photograph courtesy of the Payette National Forest.

A guided elk hunt provided by Hollenbeak's Cabin Creek Ranch. (Above) A hunter and his guide look for elk on a ridge high above the ranch. (Below) Pack string with the results of a successful hunt. Photographs from the collection of Kathy (Hollenbeak) Kough provided by Richard H. Holm Jr.

their ranches. The trip from Big Creek Village took several days and was supported by a pack string operated by Bob Gillihan. According to Cathy Gillihan, although the cat was used to put the Big Creek River back into its original channels and repair the damage to the meadows along the river for hay ground and pasture, it was used very little on the airstrip except to smooth it out and to widen and lengthen the north end of the strip. It also was driven up the river by Hollenbeak and used to build the airstrip at John Vines' place [the old Ritchey/Garden Ranch], in the 1960's.

Although Lanham and Hollenbeak were jointly responsible for developments at Cabin Creek during seven (1957-1963) of the first 10 years after Jean Wallace sold off her portion, Lanham was the prevailing force and the ultimate benefactor when operations ceased. He also reportedly was the more successful and visionary of the two. One interviewer characterized him as " . . . a big man, with big ideas and with what it takes to make them work. Contractor, bush pilot, flying service operator, rancher, resort operator, cattleman, bait manufacturer, outdoorsman, and rugged individualist . . . ."

⸺

IN RETROSPECT, it is striking that the four individual homesteads were never successful on their own. One might have expected that, especially during the homestead era when land ownership was most fragmented, the residents would band together for "the common good" — for shared assistance during such labor-intensive times as haying and branding, for sharing of garden produce, for help during medical crises and child bearing, for more-formal education of their children, for group purchases and transport, for trading off on ranch chores and oversight when another needed to be away, and for sheer social interaction and recreation. But it rarely, if ever, happened. The occupants tended to be loners by temperament or circumstance (i.e., they actually were separated in time though not in space), and to interact with more-distant neighbors (6 miles or more miles away) and then usually only in a casual way. It also is noteworthy that neither the 140-160 acres of the individual homesteads nor the combined

300-320 acres of the Wallace/Bacon and Bellingham/Abel ranches, even including the immediately adjacent Forest Service land, were sufficient to be profitable for ranching under the harsh growing conditions and long distance to markets. The Caswells came closer to being self-sufficient than any of the others that followed, except perhaps for Abel. But even the Caswells depended on off-ranch sources of income, whether it was furs or gold, to sustain them. The 1,000 or so acres available to them for use and their reduced herd sizes were more appropriate for a subsistence life style on a sustained basis than for a profit-making one. So, in the end, it is the remoteness of Cabin Creek, once thought by the Wallaces to be an asset, that was its undoing. It was in fact just too remote to function as a commercial ranching endeavor or to provide for more than basic local subsistence. Even when operated as a high-end dude ranch with flights in and out provided by the proprietor Rex Lanham, the enterprise never paid its way and counted on outside subsidies of cash and materiel to sustain it.

➤ Return to Wilderness ➤

At various times throughout its history the United States Government has acquired land through purchases, treaties, and other means. Foremost among these in the West were the Louisiana Purchase in 1803, the U.S. annexation of Texas in 1845, the Oregon Treaty in 1846, and the U.S.-Mexican war from 1846 to 1848. Until the latter quarter of the 19th century, the general policy of the federal government was to transfer ownership to states and to private entities ranging in size from railroad corporations to individuals, but it reserved the right to retain land for national purposes such as parks and forests. With the establishment of Yellowstone National Park in 1872, the general policy of land disposal began to change to one of retention by the federal government. Forest lands led the way, starting with the establishment of Forest Reserves in 1891 and a formal agency, the Forest Service, to manage them in 1905.

Eventually it became evident to natural resource managers and conservationists that certain forest lands deserved to be protected in their natural state as examples of wilderness. They understood that wilderness areas offered opportunities to relive a piece of the past and to experience conditions faced by and employ skills used by Native Americans, early explorers, fur trappers, prospectors, and homesteaders. The early proponents of the wilderness movement such as John Muir, Aldo Leopold, and Bob Marshall understood that the preservation of examples of the remaining remnants of wildlands should be treasured as places to experience our own cultural inheritance, as opportunities for the more-challenging forms of outdoor recreation (e.g., back packing, horse packing, hunting, & fishing) insulated from settlements and roads, as places of reference of undisturbed conditions for the comparative study of used and unused ecosystems, and as refugia for endangered forms of wildlife.

In the mid-1920s, the Forest Service created the first Wilderness Area (on the Gila River in New Mexico) simply by excluding roads and denying use permits. In 1929 it established administrative categories for Experimental Forests, Natural Areas, and Primitive Areas. Primitive Areas were intended to maintain "primitive conditions of environment, transportation, habitation, and subsistence, with a view to conserving the value of such areas for purposes of public education and recreation." Specifically, their purpose was to "prevent the unnecessary elimination or impairment of unique natural values, and to conserve, so far as controlling economic considerations permit, the opportunity to the public to observe the conditions which existed in the pioneer phases of the Nation's development, and to engage in the forms of outdoor recreation characteristic of that period; thus aiding to preserve national traditions, ideals, and characteristics, and promoting a truer understanding of historical phases or national progress." The Forest Service used its administrative authority to set aside these areas. Without Congressional approval, however, there was no law to guarantee their future. In addition, their size or restrictions could be compromised through political maneuvering.

Interest in establishing a primitive area within the Idaho National Forest apparently began to coalesce during the 1927 hunting season in about October when the Regional Forester for the Intermountain Region Richard H. Rutledge accompanied the newly elected Idaho Governor H. Clarence Baldridge on a horse-packing trip to examine the area. Also on the trip were several others, including Harry Shellworth of the Boise-Payette Lumber Company and Kellogg mining executive Stanly A. Easton as unofficial representatives of the two most powerful special interest groups that might oppose primitive area designation — logging and mining.

Harry Shellworth often is overlooked for his role in instigating the idea of an Idaho primitive area between the South and Middle Forks of the Salmon River and then orchestrating its successful fulfillment. Though his efforts are largely unheralded, Shellworth probably did more than anyone else to initiate, craft, and bring to fruition the establishment of the Idaho Primitive Area.

Harry was an executive with the powerful Boise-Payette Company, a staunch Republican, a consummate lobbyist and be-

Harry Shellworth with Dave Lewis in Big Creek country. Photograph from Dave Lewis Special Collection (MS Accession #2011-03), University of Idaho.

hind-the-scenes-politician, and an avid outdoorsman. Through his position, organizational skills, and outgoing personality Shellworth built up many influential contacts in Idaho and in Washington DC, including Governor Baldridge and Senator William Borah. In addition, he knew the area and its residents and went there often on

Governor H. Clarence Baldridge, Dave Lewis, and mining executive Stanly Easton at Harry Eagan's memorial on Soldier Bar during an inspection trip of the proposed Idaho Primitive Area in October 1927. Photograph from Dave Lewis Special Collection (MS Accession #2011-03), University of Idaho Library.

extended hunting and fishing expeditions over many years. By May 1937, he claimed 26 such trips into the Primitive Area country to his credit.

Shellworth's annual hunting trips into Big Creek country commonly lasted a month. In a letter to his friend Miss "Pete" Stewart, Shellworth described his planned hunting trip for 1930: "I am leaving on my annual big hunt one week from next Thursday to be away for four weeks. I . . . will go 'in' by way of Monumental [Creek] and come 'out' by way of Chamberlain Basin. . . . There will be three of us with two packers, Bill Moore and Jim Necessary, and the cook, Guy E. Fischer, six in all and our remuda will be twenty-one mules and seven horses." He planned to spend the first night at his "old camp on Roosevelt Lake," where he intended to catch a few trout for supper. "Then the next day we will start for Uncle Dave Lewis'

Ranch via Holy Terror Trail. . . . We will be at Uncle Dave's about ten days hunting Big Horns and goats." Shellworth's 1930 itinerary probably closely followed an earlier trip in 1927 with Governor Baldridge and other influential dignitaries, though the latter was more streamlined, lasting only two weeks and allowing less time for hunting goats and Big Horns. A decade later, in the postscript of a letter to his friend Stanly Easton (May 17, 1937), Shellworth claimed that the trip was pivotal in establishing the Primitive Area: "You will recall that the move for the creation of the 'Idaho Primitive Area' was originated on the trip by yourself, Governor Baldridge, Dick Rutledge, Jess Hawley, Ansgar Johnson [among others] and myself some years ago."

During the trip, Dave Lewis and possibly then forest ranger Merl Wallace hosted the group of dignitaries into Big Creek country to examine it as a potential primitive area. In a letter to his friend Ellis L. Hale, Stanly Easton wrote on October 29, 1927 shortly after returning from the trip "The two week trip . . . was a great success particularly as a sight seeing tour, we traversed nearly one hundred and fifty miles of unfrequented trails in the Big Creek and Middle Fork of the Salmon River country, we had a moving picture man along, two packs of hounds, some fifteen packers, guides, wranglers, cooks, etc, and about forty head [of] horses, visiting some of the old indian battlefields and taking pictures of importance to Idaho publicity, forest service, and State Fish and Game Department. We really traveled too much to do careful hunting although we put in three days of hard work trying to find sheep down near the Middle Fork . . . ; we should have had a week or ten days more time in which to locate the herds; trout, birds and deer were had in unlimited quantities . . ."

In the end, the two main special-interest groups of logging and mining became convinced that their operations would not be seriously affected by primitive area designation of this particular area. Merchantable stands of timber within the proposed boundaries were limited due to low tree densities, slow growth, and inaccessibility. The Idaho Mining Association assured their members that "it is not the intention of those engaged in creating this primitive area

Senator William Borah fishing on upper Big Creek in August 1927.
Photograph courtesy of the Idaho State Historical Society
(ISHS #63-219-10).

to in any manner interfere with the mining laws as contained in the
United States revised code and which apply to the forest reserve and
the public domain" (December 21, 1931 letter from Ravenel Macbeth,
Secretary-Treasurer, Idaho Mining Association to William A.
Edwards, Edwardsburg, ID).

In August 1927, just prior to the October expedition, Shellworth
also facilitated a special motor trip for Senator Borah that went
from Boise to Edwardsburg via Warren and Elk Summit. The trip
enabled Borah to fish in upper Big Creek, experience the peaceful
solitude of the backcountry, and visit with the Edwardses about life
in the area and the importance of mining. The trip was a deft move
to engage the Senator's interest and support for protecting the area
from further encroachment by development.

Although the idea of setting aside an area protected from roads
and other development had been around since the early 1920s, it had
not received much serious attention in Idaho. However, following
the October 1927 expedition, the idea quickly gained momentum,
probably through the maneuvering of Shellworth. By July 1929, a

mechanism existed nationally (the "L-20 regulations" relating to primitive areas) by which the Forest Service could preserve wild lands. Inventories had been taken as early as 1926 which identified such places in Idaho, including Big Creek Country and adjacent lands and two other locations. In the autumn of 1930, Rutledge in his capacity as Regional Forester, asked the supervisors from the Challis, Salmon, and Payette Forests to prepare reports describing the attributes of the proposed Central Idaho Primitive Area. On November 17 Rutledge took these reports to show the Governor, who apparently was enthusiastic about the idea and asked for a summary report on the area. Rutledge then wrote the supervisors asking them to solicit the needed local support. By late November 1930, Rutledge was able to supply the Governor with the letters of support, a draft proposal, and a map of the proposed boundaries. Rutledge and Baldridge recommended a large area south of the main Salmon River, including the Big Creek, Chamberlain Basin, and Cold Meadows backcountry districts, for designation as a primitive area. The area contained about 1 million acres of National Forest land, 2800 acres of State land, and 3800 acres of private land, exclusive of mining claims. On December 1, Governor Baldridge established a committee to consider and recommend action on the US Forest Service Intermountain Region proposal to establish a primitive area in central Idaho and set December 20 for its first meeting in Boise.

The Governor's committee consisted of eleven men, mostly Republicans like himself, including three state representatives and two state senators, the state Game Warden, the president of the Idaho Chamber of Commerce, the supervisor of the Payette National Forest, and a mining operator. Harry Shellworth was officially designated to head the committee. Many of the members were personal friends of his and had been on the influential 1927 Big Creek hunting trip. The committee met on December 20, 1930 to consider the draft proposal and map previously presented to the governor and represented at the meeting by Rutledge. Stanly Easton, the Bunker Hill the mining executive, and R. E. Shepard of the State Chamber of Commerce were unable to attend. R. G. Cole, secretary of the Southwest Idaho Sportsmen's Association, was in attendance and was added to the membership near the end of the meeting by consent of the committee.

At the start of the meeting, the Governor made some introductory comments about his trip into the proposed area along Big Creek in 1927 and about not wanting to step on any one's toes or to lock things up forever. Harry Shellworth stated that the idea for a primitive area had come several years before the present meeting but that it had about died out until the "Governor's trip" brought new life and impetus to the movement. S. C. Scribner, committee member and Supervisor of the Idaho National Forest presented a summary of the proposal and Regional Forester Rutledge made a strong statement in support of it.

Following Scribner's presentation, he was asked by Jean Wallace, who was in attendance and whose home was in the region being discussed, about the rights of settlers. She was told that the vested rights of settlers could not be touched but the settlers could sell their property if they wanted. It was suggested by committeeman State Representative Cowles Andrus, a farmer and stockman, that a representative of the dwellers within the proposed primitive area be asked to meet with the committee. It was felt by the committee that Mrs. Wallace "could very ably take care of the interests of these settlers and, as she was remaining in town during the winter, she could meet with the committee." However, the committee never met again and the final document encouraged buy out, by State or Federal Agencies, of lands that were being used or likely to be used for stock ranches or dude ranches within the proposed location, in order to use these lands for game propagation or recreational use.

As its final action, the committee unanimously approved the primitive area concept and asked Rutledge to revise the report to reflect their discussions and submit it to the Chief Forester, R. Y. Stuart in Washington, DC. Rutledge was joined by Scribner in writing the final report, which was approved by the Chief on March 17, less than three months from when the committee met — a testimony to Shellworth's management skill. In its final form, the Idaho Primitive Area designation discouraged road construction, grazing,

water storage, power production, logging, and agriculture and encouraged the use of the area for recreational purposes.

As the plan moved forward, the public was notified through a
variety of meetings and newspaper articles which culminated in a
feature article by Watson Humphrey in Section Two of The Idaho
Sunday Statesman on December 28, 1930, barely a week after the
Governor's committee had met. In it Humphrey extolled the vir-
tues of the proposed primitive area under the headline "They Would
Keep the State's Wildest Beauty Unspoiled."

The steps for setting the area aside largely for conservation purposes were effectively finished by the time the Wallaces acquired
their property on Cabin Creek. However, in an article published
in the January 11, 1931 edition of the Idaho Statesman in response
to Humphrey's article, Merl strongly opposed "the establishment of
a so-called 'primitive area'" citing injustices to existing land owners
whose homes and property rights appeared to be in jeopardy. Part
of Merl's concern stemmed from the belief that the proponents of
the proposal were trying to get rid of the settlers within the area by
depriving them of their federal grazing privileges, making it impos-
sible for them to make a living from ranching or horse packing, and
thus forcing them to sell their lands to the Government.

In particular, Merl addressed the assumption by proponents of
the primitive area that the included homestead lands were too mar-
ginal to support a living. He noted that "Within these proposed
boundaries are 15 or 20 ranches totaling approximately 3400 acres,
now supporting at least 200 head of cattle and approximately 150
head of horses and capable of raising from 900 to 1000 tons of hay."
He observed that most of these ranches were situated below elevations of 5,000 feet and in protected valleys and nooks where a variety of fruit and garden produce could be grown. He also argued
that, "The absence of irrigation costs, low taxes, low grazing fees
and splendid range make it possible to produce beef for . . . half the
overhead of [locations] more accessible to the markets." If it weren't
immediately apparent, subsequent developments over the next 10 to
15 years would eventually prove Merl's belief in the fiscal sustainabil-
ity of the backcountry ranches wrong.

He also complained that the people most directly affected by the proposal, the private in-holders, were not given a voice in the planning. "Nor does it appear that all our representatives in congress or senators were informed of this scheme up to November of last year. On November 10 [1930] Jean Wallace visited Senator Borah in Boise and talked with him regarding the primitive area proposal, which he then understood was to be brought up in the next session of Congress. Senator Borah at that time stated that no such action was pending and that he had no knowledge of such proposal." What the Wallaces didn't realize at the time of Jean's meeting with Borah was that primitive area designation was strictly a Forest Service decision and that no congressional action was required. Nor were they aware of Shellworth's lobbying of the Senator in August of 1927.

Merl reserved his strongest arguments for the defense of the individual entrepreneur and for states' rights. He wrote, "This country, its potential wealth and its recreational facilities, belong of right to the citizens of Idaho. But by hedging it round with restrictions and regulations made by an agency other than the citizens of Idaho, their rights in it become of little worth and it is reserved to the wealthy sportsmen." His arguments reflected a belief in the right of individuals to live lives free of governmental control as long as they do no immediate harm. Although he believed that the planned primitive area would benefit mainly the wealthy, he apparently did not feel that it was the role of Government to provide for the welfare of all citizens regardless of economic or social status. "We who live in this country, ranchers and miners, and in our humble way sportsmen and lovers of the outdoors, who each year salt deer at our own expense, keep open house for hunters and turn out to hunt them up when lost and carry them to the doctor when injured, feel that we have an interest in this country surpassing that of the sportsmen of the east and the cities." Merl concluded with a statement of his irritation about the whole affair and a vow to fight for the rights of those still residing within the borders of the proposed primitive area. Most of the residents of Big Creek country undoubtedly backed his stand.

Primitive Area designation further complicated, beyond the obstacles faced by prior occupants, the Wallaces' intentions for successful

livestock ranching. The Forest Service sought to deny them and others permits to graze federal land adjacent to their homesteads but the
Wallaces appealed to Idaho Senator Borah, who used his political clout
to reverse the action. This development indicates how the intended restrictions of Primitive Area designation could be altered through political pressure. In gratitude, the Wallaces later named their son William
Borah Wallace in honor of the senator.

When the Idaho Forest Reserve was established, mining, logging, and homesteading were still recognized as legitimate uses of
the land. By the late 1920s it had become apparent that, because of
the rugged terrain and difficult access, a large portion of the area was
not profitable for producing timber or cattle or maintaining families and was better suited for public recreation, particularly hunting,
fishing, horse-back riding, and nature study. Establishment of the
Idaho Primitive Area in 1931 reflected these realities and, though
not stated explicitly, anticipated that most of the existing private in-
holdings would eventually be abandoned or bought out by the State
or Federal Government just as Merl Wallace had feared.

A movement had begun in the late 1930s to establish designated
wilderness areas in the United States through congressional action
but these were put on hold until after World War II. In the 1950s,
increased logging and recreational use of national forests and the
relentless increase in roads that first exploded in the 1920s led to renewed public concern about the tenuous nature of protection of these
defacto wilderness areas. There was a real fear that, without some
legal guarantee of their permanency to supplement the "protections"
afforded by agency administrative decree, these areas would be lost
to development. Future events would show that these concerns were
not unfounded and would intensify in future years. In 1956, the first
wilderness bill was introduced in Congress and included an effort to
incorporate the Idaho Primitive Area. Wilderness status was seen as
even more rigorous than "primitive" and excluded even mining and
dude ranching.

The Wilderness Act, enacted in 1964, gave Congress the
authority to designate areas as National Wildernesses. The
Wilderness System began with national forest lands the Forest

CABIN CREEK CHRONICLE

Frank Church (on right), a leader of the effort to establish the River of No Return Wilderness, and his fishing companion. Photograph # Out-059 courtesy of the Boise State University Albertsons Library Special Collections and Archives.

Hikers preparing to enter the Frank Church Wilderness at the Big Creek trailhead. Photograph by author July 2012.

Boundary marker (above) and memorial plaque (left) at the Big Creek trailhead. Photographs by author July 2012.

Service had previously designated as "wilderness" (greater than 100,000 acres) or "wild" (5,000-100,000 acres) areas. In 1968, Congress began expanding the system by creating five new wilderness areas in four states.

Further progress toward an Idaho wilderness was made during the 1970s. The Forest Service began reviewing a plan by Idaho Senator Frank Church and Montana Senator Lee Metcalf to combine the former Idaho Primitive Area and the Salmon River Breaks in a single bill. That same year, a "group of four" Idaho conservationists, consisting of Ernie Day, Bruce Bowler, Frank Jones, and Mort Brigham, formed the River of No Return Wilderness Council to lobby for a 2.2 million-acre wilderness encompassing the entire area. They recruited another Idahoan Ted Trueblood, a nationally renowned outdoor sports writer, to head the group.

In 1974, the full circle of change at Cabin Creek, from wilderness through various degrees of development and back again to wilderness, was propelled toward completion when the US Forest Service purchased the private holdings from Lanham for a reputed

Remains of Lanham's lodge soon after it was incinerated, probably 1988. Photograph by Mike Dorris provided by Richard H. Holm Jr.

1.6 million dollars, in anticipation of incorporating them into the planned wilderness. Lanham was substantially aided in obtaining the generous sale price by Lloyd Dyer who served as president and CEO for Lanham's old friend Bill Harrah. Lanham leased his former property from the Forest Service for an additional two years to afford him time to remove all of his belongings, though during that time they were subjected to theft and vandalism. In the end, no residents remained at Cabin Creek but two outfitter camps continued to operate (and still do) from wall tents sequestered among the trees adjacent to the area.

In 1979 Frank Church introduced a Central Idaho Wilderness Bill that included and expanded upon the Idaho Primitive Area. The bill was passed by Congress in July 1980. The area set aside was over twice the size of the former Idaho Primitive Area and was named the River of No Return Wilderness. It is the largest forested wilderness in the continental United States. In 1984, just weeks before Senator Church's death from cancer, Congress honored him by renaming the area "The Frank Church-River of No Return Wilderness." Earl Dodds was Big Creek district ranger throughout (1958-1984) the main period of shift from primitive area to designated wilderness and oversaw many of the changes near the end.

Though Cabin Creek officially became part of the Frank Church Wilderness in 1980, most of the buildings from the Hollenbeak/Lanham era still were present in June 1982 when a US Forest Service inventory was conducted. All reportedly were in a deteriorated condition by that time. Subsequently, the Forest Service set about methodically eliminating all existing buildings and other structures to return the scene to some semblance of its original primitive state. Most of the structures were obliterated between 1988 (when 22 were still listed as being present) and 1990.

Only two buildings, from the old Wallace homestead, were retained and extensively restored in 1988 and 1989. Both buildings are from the original Caswell ranch and consist of their 1898 cabin

The "cat that buried itself" at Cabin Creek. Photograph by Mike Dorris provided by Richard H. Holm Jr.

and what is presumed to be the main part of their storehouse. A second small cabin from the Wallace era that previously had come from the Caswell ranch also was present in 1988 but inexplicably was destroyed. One other building, situated immediately adjacent to Spring Creek, which had served as a spring house for early residents and was the temporary residence for Abel and Routson called the "milk house," was destroyed by a human-caused fire on July 31, 2008. The fire allegedly was started accidentally by Forest Service personnel who were staying in the Wallace cabin.

One of the relatively modern log buildings, known as "Lanham's Motel," was dismantled in July 1990, the sections of log walls flown by Idaho National Guard helicopter to the University of Idaho's wilderness studies facility on Pioneer Creek, and the 24' x 61' building resurrected as a combination bunkhouse and classroom. The D-8 cat, that Hollenbeak and Lanham had driven in, dug its own grave. After being employed to create a couple of "landfills" of non-combustible trash and building residue, it was used to bulldoze out an excavation, then driven in and buried. However, the by now well-developed 1750-foot long by 40-foot wide landing field was "grand-fathered in" to the enacting legislation and retained, especially through efforts of the Idaho Outfitters and Guides Association and members of the aviation community.

In 1989, the Cabin Creek property and two remaining buildings were nominated for the National Register of Historic Places and are now listed by the National Park Service as part of the National Heritage Program. However, little remains to alert present-day visitors or future generations to the rich history that transpired here. It seems that the proponents of wilderness and its stewards, for all their good intentions, have given no thought to this.

In the final analysis, the return of Cabin Creek to wilderness status has been an uneasy and imperfect one. From the outset, those charged with restoration of the site have operated under a set of mixed directives and interpretations largely out of sight of public scrutiny. The Wilderness Act recognizes wilderness as an area of undeveloped land which retains its primeval character, is primarily affected by the forces of nature, has outstanding opportunities for solitude, and is without permanent improvements or human habitation. However,

Return to Wilderness: "cleanup" of the barn at Acorn Creek. Most of the pre-existing structures on public land within the boundaries of the FCRNR Wilderness have subsequently been removed, mostly by burning, as seen here. Photograph courtesy of the Payette National Forest.

it also recognizes that such areas contain ecological, geological, or other features of scientific, educational, scenic, or historical value that should be maintained and that other accommodations to local conditions also should be met. In recognition of the differing perceptions of wilderness and their varying purposes, the Wilderness Act did not establish rigid criteria or standards for Federal wilderness designation. As a result, the "rules" are sometimes the imaginings or inventions of a relatively few who view a "wilderness" as an area where there is absolutely no sign of human presence and not even bridges, trail signs, or fire rings are to be found. To others, much less stringent criteria are acceptable or desirable.

Even within the implementation and administration of the Frank Church Wilderness there are the purists who have sought to have the area cleansed of all evidence of post-Columbian humans. Others, toward the other end of the spectrum, view the historic evidence of the presence of the early trappers, prospectors, homesteaders, and ranchers as being important parts of a rich pioneer and wilderness heritage and worthy of being retained or even stabilized. Unfortunately for many, it was mainly the purist zealots who prevailed and Cabin Creek became a microcosm where this conflict played out.

Many of the former residents of Cabin Creek, from the Caswells through the early days of the Wallaces, lived a frontier life style and their experiences were representative of the challenges met by early pioneers in the region. These people and their actions were the precursors of what now passes as wilderness. In fact, the original structures and lives of the people up to the time of Hollenbeak and Lanham were totally in keeping with the spirit of the original Idaho Primitive Area, which was to maintain "primitive conditions of environment, transportation, habitation, and subsistence, with a view to conserving the value of such areas for purposes of public education and recreation." But the history of their presence and the lessons to be learned from it have been all but erased. Imposition of rigorous interpretation of the meaning of wilderness to pre-existing structures also has run counter to the original intent of the previous primitive area designation.

Even though the 1988 Payette Forest Plan provided specific direction to nominate Cabin Creek to the National Register of Historic Places, it was only in 1989 after most of the buildings had been torn down, burned, buried, or otherwise removed, that the new Forest Archaeologist was directed to do so! He nevertheless succeeded, thereby attesting to its recognized historical importance even in its isolated and altered setting.

The Central Idaho Wilderness Act of 1980 specifically identified ranch, homestead, trapper, and other cabins and structures as being of special interest for possible stabilization, restoration, or maintenance and inclusion in the National Register of Historic Places. Yet, since the area's designation as wilderness, virtually all of these structures have been removed from the landscape, nearly always by fire and commonly under the cover of an existing wildfire. Their surgical removal has been so precise that immediately adjacent trees usually have been no more than partially scorched while the structures themselves have been totally consumed. The most extensive removal in Big Creek Country was during the fire storms of Y2K (Diamond Complex Wildfire) when only Forest Service personnel were allowed to be present. Although by then only a few structures at Cabin Creek remained, the old Caswell blacksmith shop remnants were targeted and reduced to ashes as were the remains of the old Meyers-James-Homsley cabin on Cave Creek. As the Forest Archaeologist once confided to the author "The purists want to get rid of the buildings. More and more of the early 20th century evidence of early settlement in the wilderness vanishes and it is not because we do not have the Central Idaho Wilderness Act [CIWA]. It is because of the purists who couldn't care less about the CIWA and continue to 'purify' this man-created wilderness."

In an attempt to accommodate these contrasting views of wilderness, the Act also provides for certain exemptions and delayed implementation of some restrictions. In the case of the Central Idaho Wilderness Act, for example, all pre-existing landing strips on government property were allowed to remain. Along Big Creek alone there are a total of four on federal land and two on state land. This is in spite of the fact that the original plan for the entire 1.1 million acre Primitive Area expressly noted that "the development of landing fields within the area should be prohibited excepting, perhaps, two or three that may be needed for emergency landings or for fire control work. . . . If auto travel is not to be condoned, surely entrance by air should also be discouraged."

The airstrip at Cabin Creek is one of the largest in the Frank Church Wilderness and provides a short cut for entry to "day trip-

A wolf walking the Big Creek trail on a sunny spring day before the advent of a wolf eradication policy for the area. Photograph by Holly Akenson.

pers," hunters, and others intent on circumventing the long trek in. Although providing important outlets for recreational use of the surrounding country and following a long tradition for Cabin Creek, the airstrip and outfitter camps also serve to concentrate use and create problems with human waste management and over-grazing by horses. In addition, hunting and fishing pressures there are some of the highest in the Wilderness. Although removal of the historic buildings was relatively easy to accomplish and was done in a way that did not raise public indignation, elimination of the airstrip at Cabin Creek and others elsewhere along Big Creek has not met with the same success. In the 1990s, when the runway was damaged by flooding from Cow Creek, the Forest Service tried to close it permanently but the resulting outcry by "aviation-ists" and by commercial outfitters and guides caused them to back off and they are not likely to try again.

In the winter of 2013-2014, management of the Frank Church Wilderness took an even darker turn, in which Cabin Creek again played a significant part. That winter, State Fish and Game officials employed a private hunter-trapper to eliminate two wolf packs in this central Idaho wilderness because, they claimed, the packs were eating too many elk calves. Gus Thoreson of Salmon, Idaho was hired to exterminate the wolves in the Golden and Monumental packs. The Golden pack is located in the lower Big Creek/Middle Fork area downstream of Cabin Creek; the Monumental pack resides 11 miles upstream. By January 2014, he had killed nine, mainly by trapping. Strikingly, Thoreson's sporadic communications with his employers were transmitted by satellite phone rather the more primitive means of old. In collusion with this effort, the US Forest Service allowed the airstrip and cabin at Cabin Creek to serve as a base for Thoreson's activities. It seems that their zealous protection of the wilderness covers the removal of historic man-made structures and other restrictions but not the maintenance of restored native wildlife or natural ecosystem processes. The actions of these two agencies were taken surreptitiously, without the knowledge of the general public until reported by the Idaho Statesman after Thoreson began his work. The Payette National Forest has responsibility for the protection and proper management of the Frank Church Wilderness and this elimination of entire packs of wolves is directly counter to Forest Service guidelines for wilderness management. It also was done without public review and while the elk management and predator control plans the Fish and Game used to justify these efforts, were still in draft form. The action sets a disturbing precedent that one may hope will not be repeated. It is inappropriate for an area where the maintenance of wildness is a primary goal and where the natural processes of intact ecosystems should be allowed to operate in the absence of micro-management and inept solutions. Wolves are an important and integral part of wildness and of the natural regulation of populations of large ungulates in wilderness and, where necessary, should be given precedence over the desires of commercial outfitters and their privileged clients.

In spite of the shortcomings associated with actual implementation of the Wilderness Act at Cabin Creek and in the vast roadless area surrounding it, many still see them as comparatively small prices to pay for an antidote to a world of Twitter, Tweet, and Face Book; of cell phones and Ipads; and of various other forms of constant contact and instant gratification. The River of No Return Wilderness remains one of the finest relatively intact wildernesses in the conterminous United States and continues to provide much of the solitude, challenge, and primal experience its founders envisioned. And Cabin Creek continues to provide an important portal to the area and a touchstone to our pioneer and Native American history. As time progresses, this vast roadless tract of mountains, forests, meadows, lakes, and streams can only become more valuable as a temporary refuge for humans and as a point of reference for the way nature operated in the absence of modern man. Optimistically, a more holistic and reasoned view of resource management in this wilderness ecosystem will prevail in the future and the Frank Church Wilderness will rise to its full potential. Perhaps then too Cabin Creek and its historic Caswell cabin will return to the peaceful idyllic setting envisioned so long ago by the Sheepeaters and even, in better times, by Jean and Merl Wallace and the plaintive howl of the wolf will be heard again.

Then & Now

Long-term land use comparison of Cabin Creek Flat from east end facing west. (Above) Photograph taken in the early 1920s when part of the area shown (located to the left center) was being considered for a Ranger Station (to be called Point of Rocks). Photograph courtesy of the Payette National Forest. (Below) Same view in June 2013. Photograph by Charles R. Peterson.

Long-term land use comparison of Cabin Creek Flat from mid-way facing west. (Above) Scene, recorded in about 1901, includes one of the Caswell haystacks surrounded by a pole fence and one of Lu Caswell's rifles for scale. Photograph by Luman Caswell, from an album owned by his grandson Stewart Taylor. (Below) Same view in June 2013. Photograph by Charles R. Peterson.

Long-term land use comparison of barn and field south of the 1898 ranch house. (Above) Scene recorded in about 1901 by Lu Caswell. Photograph courtesy of the Idaho State Historical Society (ISHS #P1987.26.7). (Below) Post-2000 view, after drought and the Diamond Peak fire caused the loss of the needles from the conifer trees in the background. Photograph by author 2001.

Long-term land use comparison of field below 1898 ranch house viewed from the south. This was the premier field on Cabin Creek and, with irrigation from Spring Creek and the "high ditch," was capable of producing an excellent crop of alfalfa (Bill Wallace personal communication). (Above) Scene recorded in about 1901 by Lu Caswell. Photograph by Luman Caswell from an album owned by his grandson Stewart Taylor. (Below) Scene in July 2006; former irrigation ditch has become the trail. Photograph by author.

Long-term land use comparison facing north from near the southwest end of the 1898 Caswell ranchhouse. (Above) Scene recorded in about 1901 by Lu Caswell. Photograph courtesy of the Idaho State Historical Society (ISHS #P1987.26.10). (Below) Same view in May 2011. Photograph by author.

Cabin Creek valley viewed midway down the bluff between the old upper landing field and its subsequent replacement. View is south down Cabin Creek and across Big Creek to the Canyon Creek catchment. (Above) 1966. Photograph courtesy of the Payette National Forest. (Below) Same view in September 2010 by author.

⇜ References ⇝

Arnold, R. Ross. 1932. Indian Wars of Idaho. Caxton Printers Ltd. Caldwell, ID.

Baird, Dennis and Lynn. 1987. A Campfire Vision: Establishing the Idaho Primitive Area. Journal of the West 26(3):50-58.

Bennett, Lee A., Ralph A. Finn, and Sandra L. Hardin. 1982. FCRNR Structures Inventory — Cabin Creek Ranch 10VY143. Report No. PY82-212, IMACS Site Form. US Forest Service, Payette National Forest. McCall, ID.

Brown, W. C. 1926. The Sheepeater Campaign, 1879. In: Tenth Biennial Report, Idaho Historical Society, Boise, Idaho.

Carrey, John. 1968. Moccasin Tracks of the Sheepeaters. In: Sheepeater Indian Campaign (Chamberlain Basin Country). Idaho County Free Press, Grangeville, Idaho.

Carrey, John and Cort Conley. 1980. The Middle Fork and the Sheepeater War. Backeddy Books, Cambridge, ID.

Caswell, Luman G. 1895-1903. Unpublished diaries and typed transcript. Idaho State Historical Society Library and Archives, Boise, ID (MS2/437).

Caswell, Luman G. No Date. Unpublished autobiography entitled "A Short Story of My Life. 'Quotes' by Luman Grant Caswell to my daughter Louisa Caswell, now Mrs. Clem L. Hensler." Idaho State Historical Society Library and Archives, Boise, ID.

Cox, Lafe and Emma. 1997. Idaho Mountains, Our Home: Life in Idaho's backcountry. V.O. Ranch Books, Yellow Pine, Idaho.

Federal Writers' Projects of the Works Progress Administration. 1937. The Primitive Area. Pages 345-350 in Idaho — a guide in word and picture. Caxton Printers, Ltd. Caldwell, ID.

Fuller, M. 1987. Trails of the Frank Church River of No Return Wilderness. Signpost Books.

General Land Office. No Date. Land entry files (Record Group 49 Serial patents for homesteads) for Orlando Abel (No. 615566), Archie Bacon

(No. 649173), and John Conyers (No. 702326). US National Archives, Washington, DC.

Holmer, Richard N. 1990. Prehistory of the Northern Shoshone. Pages 41-57 in: Fort Hall and the Shoshone-Bannock. E. S. Lohse and R. N. Holmer editors. Idaho State University Press, Pocatello, ID.

Johnson, Barbara Wallace. (Compiler.) 2009. Wallace Family Records: Volumes 1 and 2. Special Collections Branch, University of Idaho, Moscow, ID.

Kingsbury, Lawrence A. 2007. American Indian archaeological overview for the Payette National Forest, Idaho. Payette National Forest, McCall, ID.

Koeppen, Michael H. 2011. "That night, after the moon had got down . . . ." Lt. Catley's 1879 Affair on Vinegar Hill. Payette National Forest.

Leonhardy, Frank and Fred Thomas. 1985. Archaeological research in the Big Creek Ranger District, Payette National Forest, Idaho. Laboratory of Anthropology, University of Idaho, unpublished manuscript.

Lewis, Dave. Supporting Catley was a 34-mule pack train with six civilian packers, including Dave Lewis, and two scouts Josh Faulkner and Dave Munroe [Dave Lewis' letter to W. C. Brown 2-1-1925].

McCoy, Aloha Beck (1980) and Margaret Fuller (1984). The story of the McCoy Family of Yellow Pine, Idaho. Heritage Program, Cultural Resources, Payette National Forest, McCall, Idaho.

Nielsen, Dulcimer. 1979. Hanging and Rattling; an autobiography of W. E. "Ed" James as told to Dulcimer Nielsen. Caxton Printers, Ltd., Caldwell, ID.

Parke, Adelia Routson. 1955. Memoirs of an old timer. Signal-American Printers, Weiser, Idaho.

Peek, Pat Cary. 2004. Cougar Dave: mountain man of Idaho. Ninebark Publications. Printed by Maverick Publications, Bend, OR.

Preston, Peter. 1995. Wilderness Post Offices: A History of Postal Service in the Wilderness Area of the Salmon river Mountains of Central Idaho. Heritage Program, Payette National Forest, McCall, ID.

Preston, Peter. 1998. The early days of the Idaho National Forest and the first forest rangers: 1908-1924. Heritage Program, Payette National Forest.

Preston, Peter. 2000. "Gamblers' Winnings": The Jensen [sic] brothers and the Snowshoe Mine. Heritage Program, Payette National Forest, McCall, ID.

Preston, Peter. 2001. An outline of the cultural history of the Frank Church — River of No Return Wilderness administered by the Payette National Forest. Heritage Program, Payette National Forest, McCall, ID.

Preston, Peter, Dan LeVan Jr., Aloha Beck McCoy, Bob McCoy, and Althea Mietuttunen. 2007. The McCoy Family, The LeVan Family and some of their associates in the Big Creek-Chamberlain backcountry, 1920-1950. Heritage Program, Payette National Forest, McCall, ID.

Reed, Kate O'Brien. 1989. National Register of Historic Places Registration Form — Cabin Creek Ranch 10VY143/PY-113. US Forest Service, Payette National Forest. McCall, ID.

Routson, Noel. 1997. Memoirs of an old prospector. Heritage Program, Payette National Forest, McCall, ID.

Reddy, Sheila D. 1995. American Indians of Idaho, the Payette National Forest and the Frank Church — River of No Return Wilderness. Payette National Forest, Heritage Program. 15 p.

Reddy, Sheila D. 1995. Shadows in the Wilderness: The story of the Northern Shoshoni Band, the Tukudika, in the Frank Church — River of No Return Wilderness and the Payette National Forest. Payette National Forest, Heritage Program. 22 p.

Shellworth, Harry C. Various Dates. Correspondence and annotated copies of the Draft Primitive Area Plan and typed record of the Governor's Committee meeting. ISHS MS 269. (See also Primitive Area-Shellworth file).

Utley, Robert M. 2003. The Indian Frontier 1846-1890. Revised edition. University of New Mexico Press, Albuquerque, NM.

Utley, Robert M. 1973. Frontier Regulars: the United States Army and the Indians 1866-1891. Macmillan Publishing Co., Inc., New York. 462 p.

Order Form

Streamside Scribe Press
G. Wayne Minshall, author & co-owner
1783 S. Old Highway 91
Inkom, ID 83245-1700
email: streamsidescribe@gmail.com
website: www.streamsidescribepress.com

We accept orders from individuals and supply booksellers. We offer quantity discounts on orders of three or more copies. Prices will be provided on request. Send check or money order to the above address. Include the number of copies ordered and your complete address with telephone number or email address.

31101945R00095

Made in the USA
San Bernardino, CA
02 April 2019